COME,
HOLY
SPIRIT

"An absorbing read for anyone interested in what makes a great leader great. I had not known that Fr. Hesburgh opened his heart daily to the Holy Spirit."

Fr. Dennis J. Dease
President Emeritus
University of St. Thomas

"Anyone who is familiar with the history of Catholic higher education in the 1960s and 1970s knows that one person, Fr. Theodore Hesburgh, CSC, had an enormous impact that shaped thinking on the role of theology, academic freedom, and the mission of Catholic colleges and universities. With the passage of years, his contribution can be evaluated accurately. This volume offers talks and addresses by Hesburgh that make clear his thinking on several issues, some of which continue to be debated today."

Fr. James L. Heft, SM
Alton M. Brooks professor of religion and founding director of Institute for
Advanced Catholic Studies
University of Southern California

"Fr. Ted Hesburgh has been an important part of my life since 1971 when I came to the University of Notre Dame. He always gave me hope and direction with the power of prayer and courage to believe in my faith. I honor him every day by riding by his grave and praying to him for my daily intentions. Reading this book reminds me of his grace, wisdom, humanity, and unwavering faith in the glory of God."

Digger Phelps
Former Men's Basketball Coach
University of Notre Dame

"The documents in this fine collection speak to the vitality of Fr. Hesburgh's spiritual life and are often deeply moving. The collection affords excellent insight into his storied career as an educator and crusader for social justice, and provides a superb documentary record of the sea-change in American Catholic history through which he lived. A pleasure to read."

Leslie Woodcock Tentler
Professor of History Emerita
Catholic University of America

"Fr. Ted's words provide guidance for how all of us can respond to the callings God places on our own hearts."

From the foreword by **Fr. John I. Jenkins, CSC**

COME,
HOLY
SPIRIT

SPIRITUAL WISDOM FROM
FR. TED HESBURGH

TODD C. REAM, GERARD J. OLINGER, CSC,
& HANNAH M. PICK, EDITORS

FOREWORD BY JOHN I. JENKINS, CSC

AVE MARIA PRESS AVE Notre Dame, Indiana

Founded in 1865, Ave Maria Press is a ministry of the United States Province of Holy Cross.

www.avemariapress.com

Paperback: ISBN-13 978-1-64680-115-2

E-book: ISBN-13 978-1-64680-116-9

Cover image by Bruce Harlan © Notre Dame Archives.

Cover and text design by Christopher D. Tobin.

Printed and bound in the United States of America.

Library of Congress Cataloging-in-Publication Data is available.

"The Holy Spirit is the light and strength of my life,
for which I am eternally grateful. My best daily prayer,
apart from the Mass and breviary,
continues to be simply, 'Come, Holy Spirit.'
No better prayer, no better results:
much light and much strength."
—*Fr. Ted Hesburgh, CSC*

CONTENTS

FOREWORD

John I. Jenkins, CSC
President, University of Notre Dame

On March 4, 2015, I ascended the pulpit in the Basilica of the Sacred Heart to offer the homily for the funeral Mass for Fr. Ted Hesburgh. Fr. Ted's casket lay just in front of the sanctuary, on the very spot where he was ordained a priest in the Congregation of Holy Cross on June 24, 1943. As I grieved the loss of a brother in Holy Cross, a mentor, a friend, and a model of who a priest (and University president) should be, I had the challenge of making sense of the seventy-two years which spanned the day of Fr. Ted's ordination to the day he went home to the Lord.

I admitted at that time, and this still rings true today, that while I am often faced with daunting tasks as president of Notre Dame few have been more difficult than the one before me on March 4, 2015—finding words to do justice to Father Ted's remarkable life. Making sense of the breadth and depth of Father Ted's legacy is such a daunting task, as perhaps next to Notre Dame's founder, Fr. Edward Sorin, few (if any) have had a greater impact on the University than Fr. Ted.

Fr. Ted's impact, however, reached well beyond the campus, as his counsel was often sought by popes and presidents alike. I thus had to ask—how can we sum up the life of an admired university president, a champion of civil rights, peace, and the poor, a friend of so many both great and ordinary, and someone who was always generous to those who came to him with any need? How can we draw together the strands of a life that spanned so many years, served in so many realms, and touched so many lives?

Fortunately, Fr. Ted himself has given us the answer and did so with frequency during his life—he was first and foremost a priest of God. For all the celebrated encounters and accomplishments of his life, Fr. Ted always held that the most momentous day of his life was the day of his ordination as a priest in Sacred Heart Basilica on the campus of Notre Dame. And so he went on his legendary travels, a collar around his neck and a black bag in hand bearing witness to that which defined him. For Fr. Ted, his calling as a priest was simple—he was a pontifex, a bridge builder or mediator between God and humanity, who went where God called him to go and served whom God called him to serve.

For Fr. Ted, his calling, while simple, was never simplistic. When he assumed the University presidency nine years after his ordination, he came with a vision of turning a school well-known for football into one of the nation's great institutions for higher learning. That vision not only included appointments to the faculty and the creation of great centers and institutes for scholarship and research but one that flowed from our Catholic character and which could serve also as a kind of mediator, mediating between Church and world, God and humanity, between cultures and traditions and languages. That same calling was one that compelled Fr. Ted to accept a request to serve as the Vatican's representative to the International Atomic Energy Agency, as well as Pope Paul VI's invitation to establish what became the Tantur Ecumenical Institute. That same calling also compelled him to accept President Eisenhower's request that he serve on the Civil Rights Commission and President Carter's request that he chair the Select Commission on Immigration and Refugee Policy.

To be faithful to the magnitude of this calling, Fr. Ted knew more than anyone that he needed God's grace. Daily, he committed himself to two essential tasks—celebrating the Mass, and offering these words of prayer: *Veni Sancte Spiritus*. "Come, Holy

Spirit." It was the Holy Spirit, Fr. Ted believed, that would provide the grace, wisdom, and fortitude to take on the tasks to which God had called him.

Fr. Ted never believed his was a solitary or entirely unique vocation. He believed that he was called to participate in the priesthood of Christ, along with other priests as well as lay women and men. He believed deeply in the theology that matured especially in the Second Vatican Council, which affirmed the vocation of the laity as participants in Christ's own priesthood, the People of God called to also serve as mediators between God and humanity. Together and with the Holy Spirit as inspiration, guide, and companion, Fr. Ted believed that a vocation well-lived could be truly transformative for the entire world.

What follows in this volume are expressions of the spiritual wisdom Fr. Ted sought to share over the course of his life to laypersons, vowed religious, and clergy alike. These words confirm that any effort to understand Fr. Ted must first and foremost begin with his own understanding as a priest. These words also provide guidance for how all of us can respond to the callings God places on our own hearts.

As we read these words and reflect upon the wisdom Father Ted sought to share with us, may they point all of us back to his favorite prayer—*Come, Holy Spirit.*

INTRODUCTION

Todd C. Ream, Gerard J. Olinger, CSC,
and Hannah M. Pick

Rev. Theodore Martin Hesburgh, CSC (or Fr. Ted as he came to be fondly known), was the twentieth century's most widely recognized priest and university president. That recognition came first and foremost from the way he helped transform the University of Notre Dame while serving as its president (1952–1987)—doubling its enrollment, adding 40 buildings, growing its endowment from $9 million to $350 million, and increasing student aid from $20,000 to $40 million.[1]

Notre Dame's institutional transformation represents only part of Fr. Ted's accomplishments. Filling a myriad of papal and presidential appointments, Fr. Ted's impact extended beyond the university to both civil and ecclesial circles, national and international audiences. Within the Church, Fr. Ted's contributions included serving as the Vatican's delegate to the International Atomic Energy Commission for fourteen years (1957–1970) and, at the request of Pope Paul VI, leading the construction and subsequent stewardship of the Tantur Ecumenical Institute (opened 1972) in Jerusalem—an initiative for which Notre Dame is responsible to this day.

Fr. Ted was also called upon often by the United States government, and his sixteen presidential appointments included service as diverse as the National Science Board (1954–1966) and the Clemency Board (1974–1975). He was heavily involved for fifteen years in the Civil Rights Commission (1957–1972), serving as its chair for three of those years (1969–1972). He also led the Select Commission on Immigration and Refugee Policy (1978–1981), which marked only the second and, to this day, last effort to reform immigration policy in the nation's history. In addition to this public service, Fr. Ted's expertise was also sought by entities such as the Chase Manhattan Bank (1972–1981) and the Rockefeller Foundation (1977–1982), each of which numbered Fr. Ted among its board of directors.

The recognition Fr. Ted garnered over the course of his lifetime is evident in the many accolades he received, including the Presidential Medal of Freedom (1964), the Congressional Gold Medal (2000), and memorialization on a United States Postal Service "Forever Stamp" (2017). Such recognition, which continues to this day, is understandably determined by his record of public service. This recognition, however, as well as the sheer breadth of his activities, tends to obscure the active spiritual life that profoundly nurtured Fr. Ted's identity. When asked what he was most proud of during his lifetime, Fr. Ted offered the following one-word reply: priest.

To be fair, individuals who seek to assess Fr. Ted's legacy acknowledge his record of active service was driven by his calling to the priesthood. Yet most of assessments stop at that point, neglecting to explore at a deeper level how Fr. Ted's profound spiritual life, especially his persistent prayer of "Come, Holy Spirit" and daily celebration of Mass, sustained the "long obedience" he was called upon to exercise in a myriad of directions.

First published in 1980, Eugene Peterson's *A Long Obedience in the Same Direction: Discipleship in an Instant Society* (Downers Grove, IL: InterVarsity Press) is often referenced as a contemporary classic. Part of Peterson's point was to offer people a vision for discipleship in an age of constant distraction. While our nod to Peterson's title may stand in contrast to what he intended, we, in fact, believe Fr. Ted's life is an example of much of what Peterson was arguing—in particular, the calling to serve Christ and His Church can sustain people regardless of the myriad of ways they are called to serve.

Fortunately, Fr. Ted's writings offer a rich repository for exploring the spiritual life that sustained him. This volume is intended as a first attempt at mining this repository and making the depth of Fr. Ted's spirituality available as a means of inspiration not only to priests and vowed religious, but to laypersons who also strive to live, like Fr. Ted, lives of "long obedience" in multiple directions. We also hope that it contributes to a deeper understanding of the relationship between contemplation and action, prayer and service, both in Fr. Ted's life and in the life to which all followers of Christ are called.

This volume, therefore, implicitly makes two interrelated contributions. First, it suggests that Fr. Ted's lectures and homilies offer insights that are of great benefit to the spiritual formation of laypersons. When away from Notre Dame, Fr. Ted spent the majority of his time working with laypersons to address some of the greatest challenges facing their generation. While also certainly relevant for priests, religious sisters, and religious brothers, the accessible nature of his spiritual writings will particularly encourage laypersons who strive to address the challenges facing their own generations.

Second, Fr. Ted is understandably known for his achievements on and beyond the Notre Dame campus. In addition, he is often recognized as one called to the priesthood in the Congregation of Holy Cross. However, very few individuals who have written about Fr. Ted's life have tried to grasp in great detail how Fr. Ted nurtured his calling and did so, for example, through his commitment to prayer and reflection—seen most saliently in his very public and fervent commitment to the daily celebration of the Eucharist. As a result, Fr. Ted's spiritual writings will not only prove encouraging to persons striving to address the challenges facing their own generation, but will also shed light on this underexplored facet of Fr. Ted's identity for those interested more broadly in his life and legacy.

• • •

Although published in 1946, Fr. Ted's dissertation and first book, *The Theology of Catholic Action* (Notre Dame, IN: Ave Maria Press), anticipated many of the ideals which came to fruition during Vatican II and in constitutions such as *Lumen Gentium*. When addressing the National Catholic Education Association in 1982, Fr. Ted went so far as to argue that "no one need justify today that if we are to do what the Church must do in every age, in our age, it will, in great measure, especially in education, be a work of a committed and dedicated Catholic laity, men and women. I welcome this and, as a religious priest, I rejoice at the collaboration that strengthens and assures the success of all of our educational dreams."[2]

In Fr. Ted's estimation, the diversity of expertise the laity possessed was not only to be respected but valued for what it offered the Church and educational institutions as they sought to fulfill their respective callings to meet the world's needs.

While the selections included in this volume were chosen based on their ability to demonstrate what that engagement looks like in a variety of different contexts, they were also chosen in light of their accessibility to members of the anticipated audience.

Fr. Ted was a university president and trained theologian. However, he believed the eternal truths theology communicated were applicable to any challenge plaguing humanity. As an accessible and encouraging resource for both religious and laypersons, this volume prompts readers to think more deeply about how those eternal truths relate to any number of societal challenges.

As the future leaders of the Church, this volume also prompts students to begin to think through those same questions. Hopefully, they do not view their theology classes as simply intellectual exercises. What relevance do theological truths have for our lives and the lives of those around us? What does our Christian faith have to offer a suffering world? God's truth may be simple but never simplistic. Questions concerning the Trinity, the nature of Christ, and what it means to be human, for example, are to be explored at the level of their greatest depth. However, that depth does not preclude them from being relevant to the most immediate and pressing of life's challenges.

• • •

Despite his prominence, only one volume of Fr. Ted's writings remains in print, and no volumes of his spiritual writings, in particular, were ever published. This volume thus seeks to fill that latter void while also adding to the growing number of popular and scholarly resources concerning Fr. Ted's life and legacy.

Indicative of growing interest in Fr. Ted's legacy, Patrick Creadon's *Hesburgh* was released in theaters across the country in 2017 and is now available for download and on DVD. In addition, Liturgical Press published Edward Hahnenberg's *Theodore Hesburgh: Bridge Builder* in August 2020 in its "People of God" book series. Other figures covered in that series include important twentieth and twenty-first century Catholics such as Dorothy Day, Flannery O'Connor, and the pope with whom Fr. Ted shared the closest personal and professional relationship, Paul VI.[3]

Of his own publications, only one, *God, Country, Notre Dame* (New York: Doubleday, 1990 / Notre Dame, IN: University of Notre Dame Press, 1999-HC & 2018-PB), is still in print. Fr. Ted published *The Theology of Catholic Action* (Notre Dame, IN: Ave Maria Press) in 1946 and his theology textbook, *God and the World of Man* (Notre Dame, IN: University of Notre Dame Press), in 1950. Fr. Ted then published a collection of six addresses he delivered at Notre Dame during the first years of his presidency under the title *Patterns for Educational Growth* (San Francisco, CA: Jossey-Bass, 1958). In many ways, those essays offer insights into Fr. Ted's thinking on a variety of topics related to education and thus how he would lead the university over the course of the next three decades. Later, along with Paul A. Miller and Clifton R. Wharton Jr., Fr. Ted published a volume with a broader focus related to education, *Patterns for Lifelong Learning* (San Francisco, CA: Jossey-Bass, 1973).

Perhaps the most diverse collection of Fr. Ted's writings is found in a series (five in total) of pamphlets the University of Notre Dame published and mailed directly to friends of the university. Known as "Thoughts for Our Times" and published in 1962, 1964, 1966, 1967, and 1969, those essays offer examples of Fr. Ted's thinking in those particular years on issues ranging from science and technology to human rights.

After giving the Terry Lectures at Yale University, Fr. Ted published *The Humane Imperative: A Challenge for the Year 2000* (New Haven, CT: Yale University Press, 1974). Continuing to expand the focus of his interests, the essays in that collection addressed such topics as ecumenism, civil rights, population growth, and environmentalism. In 1979, the Council on Foreign Relations and International Affairs published *Foreign Policy and Morality: Framework for a Moral Audit*. It included Fr. Ted's "Moral Aspirations and American Foreign Policy" and Louis J. Halle's "Applying Morality to Foreign Policy." Those essays were followed by commentary and reflections by John C. Bennett, George F. Kennan, John P. Armstrong, Phillip C. Jessup, E. Raymond Platig, and Kenneth W. Thompson.

In 1979, Fr. Ted also published *The Hesburgh Papers: Higher Values in Higher Education* (Kansas City, MO: Andrews & McMeel). Focused on education, that volume contains twenty-three essays broken into five sections. For example, section four, "The Years of Campus Crisis," contains lectures and forms of correspondence concerning the student unrest that took place in the late 1960s and early 1970s. Fr. Ted also published an edited collection of approximately thirty essays by a wide range of scholars in *The Challenge and Promise of a Catholic University* (Notre Dame, IN: University of Notre Dame Press, 1994). He contributed an introduction by the same title and offered a perspective gained from being seven years removed from the day-to-day demands of the presidency.

Finally, Thomas J. Mueller's and Charlotte A. Ames's *Fr. Theodore M. Hesburgh: Commitment, Compassion, Consecration*

(Huntington, IN: Our Sunday Visitor, 1989) offers a topically organized set of quotations drawn from Fr. Ted's writings, which often reflect the heart of his ideas on a wide variety of matters and over a long span of time. That work is designed to give readers an initial appreciation for the breadth and inspirational nature of Fr. Ted's thinking.

• • •

This volume includes selections from among Fr. Ted's lectures and homilies. Some of those selections include the full text, while others (especially his lectures) include excerpts. Part of what determined those selections was how they speak to the lives of the audience this volume is designed to reach. Another part of what determined those selections was how they fit together in a topical fashion.

In terms of a lecture, for example, we included an excerpt from Fr. Ted's "The Character of a Christian." Delivered as part of a series concerning the mission he believed the laity was called to pursue in the Church as defined by the characters of baptism and confirmation, Fr. Ted argued the spirit of Christ "must come not from a few priests we have in the world but from the tremendous number of good Catholic laymen, like yourselves, who realize what it is to grow in Christ, who are trying to let their baptism blossom out into the fullness of Christ in their souls."[4]

An example of an excerpted homily can be seen in "The Catholic Spirit of Christmas." Concerned about the "commercial travesty" that Christmas "had become in many quarters," Fr. Ted sought to unpack the ways Christmas is "the inauguration of a culture, the beginning of a creed, the fountainhead of man's hope."[5] As a result, Fr. Ted contended, Christmas "is a holiday only because it is first a holy day—the day on which Christ, the Son of God, became Man."[6]

In a topically organized manner, the selections included in this volume were chosen based upon their potential to encourage readers—religious and laypersons alike—striving to address the challenges facing their own generations.[7] Regardless of what challenges you are facing, we hope you find Fr. Ted's writings to be a hopeful resource concerning how, by the "Holy Spirit we may be truly wise and ever enjoy [God's] consolations."

Notes

1. "The Notre Dame President," The University of Notre Dame, https:// Fr. Ted.nd.edu/fr-teds-life/the-notre-dame-president/.

2. Theodore M. Fr. Ted, "The Catholic Church and Education"— CPHS142-19-03, 13. Theodore Martin Fr. Ted Papers (PHS), University of Notre Dame Archives (UNDA), Notre Dame, IN 46556.

3. To date, three rather concise biographies of Fr. Ted are available and two are still in print. John Lungren Jr.'s *Hesburgh of Notre Dame: Priest, Educator, and Public Servant* (Kansas City, MO: Sheed & Ward, 1987) was published the year Fr. Ted retired from the Notre Dame presidency and is no longer in print. Jill A. Boughton's and Julie Waters's *God's Icebreaker: The Life and Adventures of Father Ted Fr. Ted Hesburgh of Notre Dame* (Notre Dame, IN: Corby Books, 2011) is designed for children and is the most recent of the three biographies. Michael O'Brien's *Hesburgh: A Biography* (Washington, DC: Catholic University of America Press, 1998) then proves to be the most comprehensive biography of the three.

In addition, Joel R. Connelly and Howard J. Dooley, in *Hesburgh's Notre Dame: Triumph in Transition* (New York, NY: Hawthorn, 1972), review roughly the first half of Fr. Ted's presidency at Notre Dame. *Thanking Father Ted: Thirty-Five Years of Notre Dame Co-Education* (Kansas City, MO: Andrews McMeel, 2007) by the Thanking Father Ted Foundation and Ann Therese Palmer (editor) is a collection of letters by alumnae and others reflecting on how much Fr. Ted's leadership for coeducation meant to them over the years. Only the second of these two books remains in print.

Since Fr. Ted's death, three memoirs were written by individuals who served with him at Notre Dame. In summer 2016, Robert Schmuhl, a journalist and recently retired member of the American studies faculty, offered *Fifty Years with Father Hesburgh: On and Off the Record* (Notre Dame, IN: University of Notre Dame Press). In spring 2017, Digger Phelps, the coach of the men's basketball program for twenty years (1971–1991), published *Father Ted Hesburgh: He Coached Me* (Chicago, IL: Triumph Books). In spring 2019, Wilson D. Miscamble, CSC, a member of the history faculty and the department's former chair, published *American Priest: The Ambitious Life and Conflicted Legacy of Notre Dame's Father Ted Hesburgh* (New York, NY: Image).

As with this volume, two volumes published in 2021 sought to introduce Fr. Ted's life and legacy as being rooted in his calling as a priest and mediator. First, Todd C. Ream's *Hesburgh of Notre Dame: The Church's Public Intellectual*

(Paulist Press) does so by introducing a wide variety of audience members to how Fr. Ted's calling as a priest and mediator influenced his efforts on and beyond the Notre Dame campus. Second, Todd C. Ream's *Hesburgh of Notre Dame: An Introduction to His Life and Work* (Lexington Books) does so by introducing scholars to how Fr. Ted's calling informed his writing concerning topics ranging from nuclear non-proliferation to community service.

4. Theodore M. Fr. Ted, "The Character of a Christian"—CPHS141-02-01, 6-7. Theodore Martin Fr. Ted Papers (PHS), University of Notre Dame Archives (UNDA), Notre Dame, IN 46556.

5. Theodore M. Fr. Ted, "The Catholic Spirit of Christmas"—CPHS141-01-08, 1. Theodore Martin Fr. Ted Papers (PHS), University of Notre Dame Archives (UNDA), Notre Dame, IN 46556.

6. Theodore M. Fr. Ted, "The Catholic Spirit of Christmas"—CPHS141-01-08, 2.

7. In many ways, Fr. Ted was a product of his time, and his writing and style of speech reflect his desire to connect with the audiences with whom he was striving to communicate at that time.

PART I
LIVES OF THE
BAPTIZED

Once you are baptized all these Blessings become yours.

—*Fr. Ted Hesburgh, CSC*

In the Christian tradition, no more appropriate nor more sacred place to begin a work on the spiritual life lived apostolically may exist than baptism. As Pope Benedict XVI stated: "The rediscovery of the value of one's baptism is the basis of the missionary commitment of every Christian, because we see in the Gospel that he who lets himself be fascinated by Christ cannot do without witnessing the joy of following in his footsteps . . . we understand even more that, in virtue of baptism, we have an inherent missionary vocation."[1] Or in the words of Pope Francis, "And with the grace of Baptism and of Eucharistic Communion I can become an instrument of God's mercy, of that beautiful mercy of God. Through baptism, not only is the stain of original sin wiped clean but our most profound identity as beloved children of God is affirmed. Through the Sacrament of Baptism, we are invited, prepared, and empowered to participate in "that work which is a spiritual supernatural social work" as an active member of the Body of Christ. Through baptism, Christians testify to their need for and surrender to redemption and embrace a new identity as God's beloved children, from which further action is born as they are increasingly prepared and purposed by God.

In "The Theology of Catholic Action," Fr. Ted explores both this identity and activity in the life and role of the layperson in the Catholic Church, reflective of Christ's own life and apostolate. Similarly, in "The Character of a Christian," Fr. Ted describes how laypersons receive a likeness to Christ the Priest as well as power to undertake some of his Priestly labor. Woven throughout both pieces is the foundational, transformational act of Baptism, by which "the layman is permanently incorporated into the Body of Christ, and begins to live with the life of Christ." From here, as a member of God's faithful, the baptized can live well a life of vocation, of faith, of prayer, of learning, and of action.

Notes

1. Pope Benedict XVI, Angelus Address, October 29, 2006.

The Theology of Catholic Action
No Date

It is more than somewhat presumptuous to attempt to cover the Theology of Catholic Action in a few moments. Actually, the best we can do is to outline the problems involved, and to give what seems to us to be the headlines of the theological solution.

It might be well to emphasize right from the beginning, the tremendous importance of this theological background of Catholic Action for the priests in the movement. If our main function is to *inspire* and to *train* the laity it is to theology that we must go to find our inspirational principles and the ideals of the apostolate for which we are training the laity. We spend untold hours telling the laity what they can *do*. We might accomplish more in shorter order by telling them what they *are*. If the laity understood their providential place and function in the divine life of the Church which theology explores, it would probably be much more obvious to them what they should do by Catholic Action.

In any case, the philosophers have been telling us for centuries that *action follows life*. The theology of lay action in the Church will then be a study not so much of the action of the layman, as of his life in the Church: that divine life which comes to him from God through Christ, the life of Christ which Catholic Action invites him to give in his measure to the dying world of today, to revitalize and draw all things to Christ.

Pius XI put this basic truth very clearly when he said: "Catholic Action is inseparable from Catholic life, for there can be no life without action, and action is the most natural and spontaneous expression of life."[1] "Catholic Action," he continues, "is the Christian life lived with zeal."[2]

At the risk of oversimplification, I should like to summarize the life and function of the layman in the Church under two basic concepts: (1) that the life of the layman in the Church comes from Christ with a special consecration to the work which stems from the life of Christ on earth: the work of apostolate;

and (2) that in the lay apostolate, the layman is, in his own way, partaking in the very apostolate of Christ himself, building up the body of Christ on earth.

To break it down into even simpler terms, Christ has given us his own redemptive work as an *objective*, basic pattern for the lay apostolate, as for all apostolates, and he has, moreover, given to the layman a specific *subjective* preparation for his participation in this apostolate of Christ. Here again we have action and life, the action and the life of Christ as our central theological reality, and the layman's high dignity as partaking in this life and action of Christ in the Church. Now to discuss these basic concepts in more detail. . . .

We must begin with Christ, for our theology of Catholic Action is specifically Christocentric. We must understand the vital importance of the Incarnation and redemption to the every-day world, if we are to understand the vitality of the Christian layman in the world today. For the layman, as well as the priest, partakes of the divine life brought to earth by the Incarnation, and hence the layman too must partake of the divine work of redemption, the Calvary and the Easter and the Pentecost which followed the Christmas of the Incarnation. "The Word was made flesh and dwelt amongst us . . . full of grace and truth . . . and it is of this fullness that we have *all* received."[3] As Pius XI says when speaking to the laity, "Each receives, each ought in his turn, to *give*."[4]

To understand what the layman is giving, what divine action he is participating in, we must go back beyond the Incarnation, to the bosom of the Most Holy Trinity, whence the Son, eternally proceeding from the Father, proceeded in time to bring this divine life of God into the world, to initiate the first apostolate by reuniting God and sinful humanity in his own Person. This is the basic mystery of Christianity that St. Paul announced to his dying breaths the key to the life and work and fecundity of the Church in which the layman participates through Catholic Action. As St. Paul puts it: "He [Christ] is the Head of His Body, the Church, He who is the beginning, the firstborn from the dead, that in all things He may hold the first place. For it has pleased God the Father that in Him [Christ] all His fullness should dwell, and that through Him [Christ] He should reconcile all things to Himself."[5]

In the third part of the *Summa*, St. Thomas teaches us that Christ in his very constitution as God-man was consecrated the unique and perfect high priest of all time. Proceeding from that basic theological fact, the Angelic Doctor sums up the work of Christ's redemptive priesthood as one of mediation: "To unite men perfectly to God belongs to Christ, through Whom men are reconciled to God . . . 'for God was truly in Christ, reconciling the world to Himself.' And so Christ alone is the perfect mediator of God and men, insofar as He reconciled the human race to God by His death."[6]

You have heard a great deal in the introductory conferences about the basic problem of the world today: a redemptive problem of mediation, a priestly problem of reuniting the things of God and the things of man, the spiritual and the temporal, time and eternity. We must never forget that *this problem has already been solved by Christ*. Objectively, the work has already been done. Our problem is to apply this work of redemption, to participate in Christ's work today, or more simply in the pontifical motto of Pius X: *instaurare omnia in Christo*. "To restore all things to Christ," he says, "has always been the motto of the Church, and it is ours particularly, in these perilous times through which we are passing."[7] Anticipating Pius XI by some twenty years, he adds: "This ensemble of works—to restore all things in Christ, all things in the family, the school, in society,—this ensemble of works of which the Catholic laity are the principal support and promoters is ordinarily designated by a special and very noble title: Catholic Action."[8]

Christ then must always be at the very *center* of our theological structure for Catholic Action. His life and his work must be our pattern. As priests, it is his priesthood that we are participating in. It is his priestly work of apostolate that we are prolonging today. But it is not exclusively ours. Christ has given the clergy a special place in the apostolate, but not a monopoly. From the Holy Father down to the humblest layman, there is a place for each in Christ's work and in Christ's kingdom. While we must apply analogy to this participation in Christ's work on the different levels of the Church's ranks, we must never forget that *Christ is at the center for all*, and all receive what they have from him. It is his life, his work, his priesthood, and his apostolate.

This is why the Holy Father could say in all truth:

> The field of Catholic Action is as vast as that of the hierarchical apostolate. Just as the hierarchical apostolate was confided to the Church, to the Bishops and to Priests for the expansion of the Reign of Christ, for the salvation of souls, for the glory of God and for the honor of Holy Church, so also, in all of these domains, a field of action is open to all the laity, who, fully conscious of their duties to God and the Church, wish to consecrate their activity to the service of the Lord and their brethren, at the side of the Bishops and Priests, under the direction and discipline of the hierarchy, that is to say, those who in our day continue the work of the Apostles.[9]

This is the objective background of the work of Catholic Action, the high dignity of the layman who really lives and works with the Church. Once more, we have the inspired word of Pius XI to summarize and conclude our first basic concept:

> What does Catholic Action wish to be? To take full account of it we must relate it to the full objective meaning of the word *Catholicism*. Catholicism means the plenitude and perfection of Christianity with Jesus who has wished it, and with the Church, who aided by Jesus Christ, works to propagate it. This is why Catholic Action signifies action in the perfection

> and plenitude of Christianity, according to the will
> of Jesus Christ, translated into the legislation of the
> Church. Hence you can understand how your mis-
> sion is to execute all according to the mind, desires,
> and precepts of Jesus Christ. In all we do, let us make
> Jesus Christ the term of every action, of every man-
> ifestation of life and thought and desire. . . . And do
> not fear, the Redeemer is with us. We are all in his
> wonderful hierarchy. Jesus Christ is with us and we
> are but instruments in His Hands. . . . It is a great
> comfort, a great grace to collaborate, when our col-
> laborator is Jesus Christ Himself.[10]

. . . Once this objective pattern of Catholic Action has been established, the second basic question is: How are the laity prepared
to participate in the priestly redemptive work of Christ? Some
talk as though the bishop merely tells them to do something,
and there you have the whole thing: Catholic Action. I do not
mean to underestimate the mandate of the bishop. It is absolutely
necessary because Catholic Action is an official external action
in a hierarchical society and, therefore, must have the sanction
of those who govern this society.

But there is a deeper, ontological reality which enables the
laity to partake in the apostolate of Christ, a consecration and
commission which comes directly from Christ himself. This
reality, called the sacramental character, constitutes the inner
subjective preparation of the layman for a participation in the
priestly redemptive work of Christ.

Again, St. Thomas gives us our lead. The objective work of
the apostolate is a work achieved once for all by the one unique
and universal priest, Christ Jesus. Those who would partake in
his priestly mediation must first be configured to his priestly
likeness and empowered to do his priestly work. According to
St. Thomas, these are precisely the effects of the sacramental
characters.

As configuration to the priesthood of Christ, "All the faithful
are deputed to receive or to give to others those things which
pertain to the service of God; and it is for this that the sacramental character is properly deputed. For the whole rite of the
Christian religion derives from the Priesthood of Christ. And
so it is evident, that the sacramental character is especially the
character of Christ to whose priesthood the faithful are configured by the sacramental characters, which are nothing else than
certain participations in the priesthood of Christ derived from
Christ Himself."[11]

As to the priestly power conferred by the characters, he is no
less explicit: "The sacramental character is a certain participation
in the priesthood of Christ in His faithful, that as Christ has the
full power of spiritual priesthood, so His faithful are configured
to Him in this, that they participate in some spiritual power
with respect to the sacraments and those things which pertain
to divine service. And for this reason, Christ does not have the
character, but the power of His priesthood is compared to the
character, just as that which is full and perfect (is compared) to
that which to some extent participates in it."[12]

The characters then, are the point of contact between the
objective redemptive work of Christ, and the prolongation of
that work in the world by Christ's members on earth.

St. Thomas further teaches that "the character is in the soul
as a certain instrumental power."[13] Thus we can conclude in general, that the exercise of all participated priestly work will have
to conform to the pattern of the principal cause, Christ, the high
priest of all redemption. The Angelic Doctor further specifies
Christ's pattern of priestly mediation: "Insofar as Christ is man
it belongs to Him to join men to God by proffering the precepts
and gifts of God to men and by sacrificing and interceding for
men to God."[14] Here is a beautiful pattern for lay spirituality,
collaboration with Christ in work and prayer. Here, too, in brief
is the work of the Church today for which the laity are prepared
by the sacramental characters of baptism and confirmation. It

is essentially a work of participation in the two great priestly actions of Christ's Mystical Body, the *ora* and the *labora*, the public prayer and universal apostolate. Here are the cornerstones of the Liturgical Movement and Catholic Action.

To delve further into the theology of Catholic Action necessitates a few words on the specific characters of Baptism and Confirmation for these are the structural sacraments that give a layman his permanent status in the life and work of the Church.

Baptism gives the primary consecration, for by the character of Baptism the layman is configured to the likeness of Christ the priest and given the passive power of receiving the fruits of Christ's priestly mediation through the reception of the other sacraments. Hence Baptism is the basic preparation for the liturgical movement, which is of tremendous importance in building up in the layman the spirit of Christ which must be diffused through Catholic Action. Baptism has another very basic relationship to Catholic Action which has been cogently expressed by the Holy Father.

> Although it is less evident to the un-theologically minded, Baptism also imposes the duty of the apostolate, because it is by Baptism that we become members of the Church, that is the Body of Christ. Among the members of the Body—and it is the same for any organism—there must be a reciprocal communication of life: 'We being many, are one Body in Christ and every one members one of another.' One member should help the other. None can remain inactive. Each receives; each ought in his turn to give. Now each Christian receives the supernatural life which circulates in the Body of Christ, this abundant life which Christ, as he said, came to bring upon the earth. And consequently, every Christian ought to pour out this life upon others who do not possess it, or who possess it only in appearance.[15]

By the baptismal character the layman is permanently incorporated into the Body of Christ, and begins to live with the life of Christ. Now since action follows life, the official apostolic *action* of the Mystical Body will follow all the formalities of *life* in the Mystical Body—it will be essentially religious, social, corporate activity. It will be hierarchically organized and specialized according to one's position in the Body. All its inner dynamism will be ultimately directed toward the good of the whole Body that Christ may be all in all, that all may grow up in Christ. These, then, are the notes and characteristics of Catholic Action, for they are primarily and fundamentally the lineaments of Catholic life in the Mystical Body.

But Baptism is only the beginning of the Christian life, as St. Thomas says: "In Baptism the Christian is made capable of what pertains to his personal salvation, insofar as he lives for himself alone. Whereas in Confirmation, the Christian attains maturity and receives the power of extending his activity to others, while before he lived for himself alone."[16] Thus Confirmation perfects what Baptism begins. Once more from St. Thomas, "Baptism regenerates a man in the spiritual life which is his individual life . . . but confirmation looks beyond personal sanctity to the external combat to which man is exposed."[17] Confirmation therefore brings to the layman a fuller participation in the priesthood of Christ, and gives him the fullness of the Holy Spirit as his spiritual weapons in the apostolate of the Body to which he is now a confirmed and mature member.

In this marvelous way, the layman is inwardly prepared to take his place in the life and work of the Church. Like all living bodies, the Mystical Body of Christ has its immanent and transient action, grows inwardly and outwardly through the great priestly works of prayer and apostolate. What we must emphasize for the laity is that this life and growth of the Mystical Body is a *corporate* reality in which all of them have a vital part, to which all of them are perpetually committed by their configuration to the priestly head of the Body. Thus all baptized and confirmed members of Christ are empowered to continue in every age and in every place the great priestly work which he initiated—to bring men to God and God to men.

Our task as priests is to inspire every Christian to collaborate effectively with Christ and the Church in this magnificent work of redemption. What better way of doing this than by telling the layman what he *is* in Christ. If we can get the laity to appreciate their God-given place in the *life* of the Church, I do not think we shall have too much trouble getting them to consecrate themselves heart and soul to the *work* of the Church, to the restoration of all things in Christ.

Notes

1. Pius XI, "Address to the Pilgrimage of 'France du Travail,'" May 20, 1929, *Documentation Catholique*, 144.

2. Pius XI, "Address to the Pontifical Work of the Missions at Rome," April 29, 1938, E. Guerry, *L'Action Catholique*, p13, n. 20 bis.

3. See John 1:14–16.

4. Pius XI, "Ex Officiosis litteris" (to Card. Carejeira), November 10, 1933. A.A.S., Series II, Vol 1:629.

5. See Colossians 1:18–20.

6. St. Thomas, *Summa Theologica*, 3.26.1.c.

7. Pius X, "Address to the Young Catholic Women of Belgium," August 26, 1933, *Documentation Catholique*, 456.

8. Pius X, 456.

9. "Address to the Bishops and Pilgrims of Yugoslavia," May 5, 1929, *Documentation Catholique*, 139.

10. Pius XI, "Address to the Committee of Italian Catholic Action," April 9, 1924, *Documentation Catholique*, 89–90.

11. St. Thomas, *Summa Theologica*, 3.63.3.c.

12. St. Thomas, *Summa Theologica*, 3.63.5.c.

13. St. Thomas, *Summa Theologica*, 3.63.5.l.

14. St. Thomas, *Summa Theologica*, 3.26.2.c., ad finem.

15. Supra, n. 4.

16. St. Thomas, *Summa Theologica*, 3.72.2.c.

17. St. Thomas, *Summa Theologica*, 3.72.4., ad 3.

The Character of a Christian
July 13, 1951

This problem of what is the mission of a layman in the Church will certainly have to depend on a layman's status in the Church. I think too often we hear it said that a layman should do this and a layman should do that. Everyone has some suggestion about what a layman should do in the Church, and too often we are talking about peripheral jobs, jobs that may seem like jobs for an errand boy or a third assistant. At times, we cloud the issue by not getting down to just exactly what makes a layman what he is in the Church.

Having studied this problem for some time, I think we can reduce it to something permanent that all of you have as Catholic layman. That something permanent is something that you received when you were baptized and when you were confirmed. You have heard about it in catechism. They call it a character. Every man in this room who has been baptized and confirmed has two characters—the character of Baptism and the character of Confirmation. Anything that you are in the Catholic Church in a permanent way will stem from those two characters and what they mean, and the next obvious question is, what do they mean?

One of the greatest theologians of all times, St. Thomas Aquinas, has written quite a bit about this character, Baptism and Confirmation, as well as the character of Priesthood, or Holy Orders. He says there are two things that make up the real meaning of a character. The first is that the character gives you a configuration or likeness to Christ the Priest and a commitment to do his work, and secondly, the character gives you the power as laymen to do some work of Christ the Priest.

This may seem confusing because you may say by definition, we are laymen and not priests—how then can our position in the Church be explained by this character which gives us a likeness to Christ the Priest—a commitment to his task with the power to do something in collaboration with him as the Head of the Mystical Body of the Church. I believe the answer would go back a long way. It would be something that was said in the first talk of this series. Fr. McDonagh reminded you that our Holy Father Pope Pius XII in one of his elocutions to the laity remarked, "You do not belong to the Church, you are the Church."

In other words, the Church is the Body of Christ and you are just as much a member of that Church as I am. You are just as much a member as the pope, or your Bishop or as anyone else in the Church, because if you are a member of this Body you have to live the life that runs throughout the whole Body. You have to be committed to the same good as every other person in that Body. You have to have the same means and the same tasks at hand and somehow you have to collaborate as a member of that Body with everything that is going on in it.

This leads us very quickly to the second question: what is the life of the Body which you as laymen have a direct part? Let me digress for a moment into some psychology. One of the greatest things studied in psychology is life. There are two kinds of activity that characterize life. (I may sound a little pedantic in this, but once we lay the groundwork, I think the conclusion will be obvious.) The first kind of activity is an imminent self-perfecting activity, the kind of activity that physically you call metabolism; intellectually, you call getting an education; or spiritually, you would call growing up in Christ.

There is within every living body an internal, self-perfecting action, which is a sure sign of a body that is alive and not stagnant or dead or decomposing. Besides this imminent, self-perfecting activity, that goes with everybody, there is an external, transient activity whereby the perfection of the life or the body is transferred to other people. A good example of this would be a man teaching from the store of wisdom he has—transmitting this perfection to other people after building it up in himself through his own education. Another idea would be parenthood where husbands and wives pass on their physical life to their children and then further educate their children from their own intellectual and spiritual lives.

Now then if the Church is the Mystical Body of Christ, it has to have two kinds of activity—the one kind of activity must be a self-perfecting, growing up activity, and the other must be the activity that carries the body in all its effects, goods, and blessings out to the world around it. In a word these two activities which characterize the life of the Mystical Body are the prayer and the work of the Body, what are called in Latin the *ora* and the *labora*. If these are the real works that characterize the body you, as layman, must somehow have an active part in both of these works if you are to be a real living member, if you are the Body of Christ.

Now then, how are you prepared for those works? Can you actually take part in both of those works, that self-perfecting work that goes on in the Body of Christ, that growing up with Christ, that union with Christ, that being united with Christ? Can you have a real active part in that? Secondly, can you have a work in, or a participation in the transient work of the body, the carrying of the spirit and the influence of Christ out to the world around you?

If anything has been emphasized by the Popes of the past twenty or thirty years, especially Pius X, Pius XI, and our present reigning Pius XII, it has been this: the laymen of today cannot merely be a dead member of a living body. If the Church is to grow today it has to grow the way every other body grows by its internal perfection of all the members and by the carrying of that perfection to others in blessings. You can't do that work which is a spiritual supernatural social work just because someone tells you to do it. My standing here and saying that it is part of your mission in the Church to do this work doesn't give you the inner preparation to do it. We are talking here about a supernatural work, about spiritual work, about work that you have to be prepared to do, the same as I have to be prepared to teach. You can't do it just because a priest or a bishop or even the pope tells you to do it. Somehow internally in your soul you have to be prepared to take part in these two great works of the Church, and I would like to tell you today that you are prepared by the fact that you have these two characters of Baptism and Confirmation engraved upon your soul.

First of all, take the character of Baptism. We are told that like all the characters, it engraves your soul to the image of Christ the Eternal Priest. Here again we can avoid a great deal of confusion because very often Catholics hear that somehow they are priests, and people say, "Well don't get it mixed up, you are not wearing a Roman collar, you are not a priest in that sense, you're getting it all mixed up, just be a layman and let it go at that." Well God didn't let it go at that, God gave you a configuration to the priesthood of Christ. How can we understand it? I think we can understand it only by understanding what the priesthood is and how the work of the priesthood, which is the work of Christ, goes on in the Church today.

Christ became a priest when his divinity, his divine nature, was joined to his human nature in the womb of the Blessed Virgin Mary. On the Feast of the Annunciation when she agreed to become the Mother of God, when the Word became flesh and dwelt amongst us, a tremendous thing was done. The divine nature, divinity came down to earth and became one of us. We say, The Word became Flesh because it was the Second Person of the Blessed Trinity Christ Jesus, who became man. And when he became Man, or his humanity, this man became the eternal priest. Why? Because a priest is essentially a mediator, he is one who stands between two extremes and joins them within himself and Christ does just this, because in his person he joins the two greatest extremes, you might say time and eternity, God and man, divinity and humanity.

He joined in his very person these two great realities of divinity and humanity, God and man, because that was the characteristic note of what he came to do as the eternal priest—He came to extend his arms and to bring all humanity in union with

God, and, as St. Thomas tells us, a priest is called *sacerdos*—"one who gives sacred things, one who brings the prayers of man to God, and one who brings the Blessings of God to man." A priest is one who stands between Heaven and earth, a man who must be close to God and must be close to men, a mediator who brings the blessings of God to men and the prayers of men to God.

Now then, Christ is the only real priest, the only eternal priest, the only real high priest. Why is this? Because he alone in his person unites the two things he came to unite in his work, he alone unites man and God in his person. And if you look at the whole work of Christ which followed the Incarnation, you will find that it is just that. It is to follow man throughout the world that Incarnation took place in his person; it is to bring all the things of man, man's work, man's marriage, man's daily life of prayers and sacrifice—to bring all the things that are close to a man's heart into contact with God and with salvation and redemption. It is to make the Spirit of God and the Spirit of faith incarnate in all the things of time. It is somehow to draw all the creatures of the earth into one vast liturgy and to offer them to God, and to seek God's blessing upon them so that they might make man happy, and they might contribute to man's salvation and redemption.

Christ did this perfectly by his work, but the fact that he redeemed all mankind doesn't mean that all men are going to be redeemed, or that all men are going to be saved, or that all people are going to heaven. He meant that the work that he did as great high priest was to be participated in by many other people, indeed, by all people of all time. To do this work and to carry on the work of incarnating God in the things of men, he established a Church which in a sense again is patterned after his own Incarnation, because the Church is the great Body of Christ, of which he, the Divine Son of God, is the head, and we, so many human elements, are the members.

Now we aren't all in the same function within that Body, we aren't all hands and feet, as St. Paul says, or all eyes and ears.

We, all of us, have something to do for the good of that Body, and because all of us have to take a part in this great work of the priesthood, of bringing God and man together, of joining the things of man and the things of God, a work that is the very opposite of secularism which separates God and the things of man. Because we all must have a part in this, the very first thing that happens when a person is made a member of the Body of Christ through Baptism, is that person is given a Character, an indelible mark on his soul which engraves upon your soul the eternal effigy of Christ, the high priest, and you are given a part to partake in the work of Christ's priesthood.

What are those works? They are only the works we explained earlier, the Works that take place in the Church, the great internal work of the Church which is to grow up in Christ, to become more Christlike, to receive the blessing of Christ's redemption in our soul, and the souls of those around us. And secondly the diffusion of that blessing, the diffusion of those graces, the bringing out of the Spirit of Christ to our work-a-day lives, into our family, into our office, into our profession, into our recreational life, into our educational life. This is the work of the Church, and this is merely the continuation of the work of Christ, the incarnating of the Spirit of the things of God and the things of man, and this is the work which you are empowered to participate in by these two great characters that go with every Catholic layman, the character of Baptism and Confirmation.

St. Thomas says that the character of Baptism gives you a power that is more passive than active because you are baptized as a child, and when you are baptized you are given the power of receiving all the good things of Christ, all the other Sacraments are opened to you. You can't really participate in the Mass and in the great liturgical acts of the Church until you are baptized. Once you are baptized all these blessings become yours. You are mentioned and remembered in every Mass. You can participate actively with the priest in carrying out the liturgy. You join and are made a part of that great internal work of the Church which is to grow up in Christ and become close to Christ, the head of the Mystical Body. You will become a member of this great social organism spread through the world, and every blessing that is diffused throughout the Church is your blessing, comes into your life and your soul. Every time the priest says his Office, praying the official prayer of the Church, you are remembered and you are a part of that prayer. In every Mass that is offered up, you are a member and you are part, because it is a Sacrifice of all living and dead Christians.

I said the character of Baptism is mainly passive, because it is the power to receive the Things of Christ, and yet it is active to this extent, that by it we are meant to work with the great liturgical action of the Church. We are not meant to sit back when Mass is going on, but to offer it up with the priest. We are to bring our lives and all they are, our work, our family life, our ideals, our troubles, day by day, the sacrifices we must make because we are Christians, the daily tensions, the burden and the heat of living in a secularistic world where so many things are against us, and so often the odds are weighted against us. We are to bring these to Mass as a great living sacrifice, so that our little gift is consecrated and sanctified with the great gift of Christ on Calvary that it might be offered up to God as a great hymn of praise. We offer our whole lives and all they mean. And this you can do because you are baptized, because you have the Image of Christ the High Priest in your soul, because you have the power to participate in this great work of priesthood which is a work of prayer, offering all the good things of men to God in prayer and praise. This is how you are associated with all the ordained priests of the Church. They offer this in your name and you offer it with them.

There is another character, the character of Confirmation. By this character we are told in theology, by St. Thomas who did it so beautifully, there is deepened within your soul, when you are Confirmed, the Image that you bear to Christ the Priest. Because Confirmation is a sacrament of adulthood in the Church you are no longer given merely the power to receive the good things of Christ, but to carry those good things to other people. In Baptism you were geared to the great inner work of the Church so that you might grow up in Christ.

We don't any of us grow up in Christ merely for our own good, but that we might bring Christ to other people, that we might bring the great incarnating Spirit of Christ into our work, into our daily lives, and our family and our professions. For that reason you have the power of the Sacrament of Confirmation. This is not merely a passive power to receive but an active power. St. Thomas says the power that comes to you through the Sacrament of Confirmation is something that stands between the power of Baptism and the Power of Holy Orders. He says that by Baptism you are geared to receive the good things of Christ, by Holy Orders or Ordination a man is geared to give unselfishly of himself to other people. And in Confirmation he says the layman is set up in the Church to bring the good things of Christ to other people, to defend the faith, to spread the faith, to be a witness to the faith.

So you can see by Confirmation, as the Holy Father keeps reminding us, you are consecrated, set aside, empowered to carry on this great external work of the life of the Church, this work of carrying Christ to other people, this great work of apostolate. So you can see when the pope says, "You do not merely belong to the Church, you are the Church," he is only saying that you as Catholic laymen have an active living part in the active life of the Church, that just as the Church is a social body, with social and religious activity, so that is your activity as well as mine.

The Holy Father does not say, "Do this because I tell you to do it, but he says do this which you have the power to do by what you have in your souls." He says, "If you carry about in your souls engraved upon them the Image of Christ the Priest, take part in this great priestly work of Mediation, by your active participation in the Liturgical Acts of the Church, take part in receiving all the Blessings that come from Christ in His Redemption." Take part in that active work of the Church, in any way you can. Take part in this great mediation of Christ, for you stand between Christ and the world you live in. Bring Christ to that world.

Take the power of Christ which you have by your Sacrament and your character of Confirmation, to be a vital, militant Catholic. Don't say that it is merely the ordained priests in the Church who have an apostolate. You have an apostolate, you are consecrated and committed to an apostolate. You have a power to do apostolic work. The Church must grow in you and through you. Baptism gives it a chance to grow in you, Confirmation a chance to grow through you.

You might ask yourselves today, "Do I want to know what kind of a Catholic layman I am?" You might ask yourselves, "How effective have the Sacraments of Baptism and Confirmation been in my life? Has the Church really grown, blossomed in my soul?" Secondly, "Has there been a normal sign of that growth, that after blossoming in my soul it has spread itself out through my carrying the influence of Christ to a world which will die without Him, to a world that is in sad need of redemption and which cannot be redeemed without Christ?"

You see the world after original sin was completely separated from God. Original sin was a barrier to be broken down. Somehow manhood and divinity had to be reunited—that reunion took place in the Incarnation, when Christ, the Second Person of the Blessed Trinity, became man, and then by his work culminating on Calvary, that union was solidified for all mankind. As I have said earlier—the work was done but still the work goes on, and it is because the work must go on that we have a Church. Because the work goes on in and through the Church, that is why everyone in the Church must help it grow.

Everyone in his own part, in his own way, must carry on the work of Christ, which is a great work of mediation to stand between God and man. To lift your prayers to the whole Mystical Body of Christ, to join your sacrifices to all the members of Christ and to let them rise in praise of God, and then to derive from God all the blessings you do derive from all your prayers and sacrifices and to carry them outwardly to men, and to your lives and to your work.

This, I think, is the greatest dignity that a Catholic layman has—to know that what he is doing as a Catholic layman is not being done just merely because some priest says, "It would be nice if you did this," or if the bishop said, "It would be nice if you did this," or if the pope says, "The world will be in a bad way if you don't do this." You do what you do because of what you are. Your place in the Church does not come from the pope, or from the bishop or from the priest, it comes from what God has given you in these sacraments, and God himself effects the work of the sacraments.

It is true, of course, that we do have external authority in the Body of Christ and that is why, since we are all working together, and the pope has put the bishops over the Church to carry out his work in the various dioceses in the world, that in your external official Catholic action you have to work hand in hand with the bishops and the priests. But, it is a work of collaboration, and just as the priest does his work because of the character of Holy Orders which he has, you are doing your work because of the character of Baptism and Confirmation which you have.

You can be just as proud of your preparation as he can of his, because while you participate in the priesthood of Christ in the lowest degree, and the priest himself also participates to a higher degree, and the bishop to a still higher degree, all of us popes, bishops, priests, and laymen, are participating in the work of the one High Priest, the Work of the one Redeemer, the work of the one Head of the Mystical Body. It is his priesthood, and there is never a priest, and there never will be a priest in this whole wide world, who is not a priest because he participates in the work of Christ the one High Priest. Christ is the Father of all priesthood. He is the beginning and the end of all priestly work, and all of us priests and laymen are participating in that work, even though to a different degree.

So I say to you today that I think this group has a double honor for not only are you doing a work which can be very close to the heart of Christ by promoting the education and welfare of the ordained priest-to-be, but at the same time you can remember that in promoting the education and welfare of young men who will be ordained priests someday you are indeed bringing the blessing of Christ's priesthood to these men. You indeed are being mediators in your own right, and you indeed are doing a priestly work in a double sense, in that you are making priests, and you are making it possible that young men may become priests, and also you are extending the kingdom of God by extending the workers and officers in his ranks.

I would like to close this talk this afternoon by asking you to meditate once in a while on the two great Sacraments of Baptism and Confirmation. In the Church we often think of Confession, Mass and Holy Communion, and possibly Marriage as being the sacraments which come closest to us, but always remember that the two Sacraments of Baptism and Confirmation have given each of you something that you will never lose. For eternity, and it will be an even greater pride when you are able to see it and realize it as you will in eternity, one of your greatest prides will be that you carry about within you the effigy of Christ, the Priest, and you realize deep in your heart that you have been committed by this effigy to carry on the work of his priesthood, that there is nowhere that you go that you cannot bring with you the Spirit of Christ, that there are many places you go that will never know the Spirit of Christ, unless it comes to this place through you, that the Spirit of Christ begins in your family with you, that the Spirit of Christ may never be in your business except through you, that the Spirit of Christ that must come to the world today, if secularism is not to overwhelm us, must come not from the few priests we have in the world, but from the tremendous number of good Catholic laymen, like yourselves, who realize what it is to grow up in Christ, who are trying to let their Baptism blossom out into the fullness of Christ in their souls and who do not hoard that fullness to themselves, but spread it out in a priestly, mediatorial way to the world which will die without it.

God bless you.

PART II

LIVES OF VOCATION: PRIESTS AND LAITY

The particular point I would highlight here is that no one is unimportant in the Church, because all of us have the same basic dignity as members of Christ, partakers of His divine life. All truth, all grace, all power, all dignity in the Church, from Pope to peasant, is from Christ. And because we share His life, we also share His work of redemption, not all in the same measure, but all truly participate if the redemptive work is to be accomplished as He wishes.

—*Fr. Ted Hesburgh, CSC*

A principal conviction grounding much of Fr. Ted's spiritual writings is his belief in the undeniable divine calling on the lives of both priests and laity to participate actively in the life of the Church and the redemptive work of Christ. While set apart for different roles within this work, layperson and priest alike are invited into—and held to—lives of humility, obedience, sacrifice, mercy, community, and conviction. These callings are in no way free from trial, frequently facing inner doubts and frustrations, interpersonal conflict, and external opposition and temptation from a world at odds with this calling in every way. However, with the promised presence of God, the caring intercession of the Blessed Virgin and the advocacy/gift of the Holy Spirit, to live and serve as a priest or a layperson is made not just possible, but truly glorious and life-giving.

Passionate about his own vocation as priest, Fr. Ted spoke at St. Francis Parish and in his "Reflections on Priesthood" of this role as one of mediation: the work of bringing God to man and man to God. His love for and belief in the priestly calling shows also in the defenses and examinations he offers in his Address to the National Federation of Priests' Councils. On the subject of laity, Fr. Ted proved no less engaged, dedicated to championing strong Christian marriages and families against what he identifies as destructive social forces. This section concludes with a focus on the layperson's role and responsibility within the Church, as well as the theology essential to empowering lay believers to carry out their earthly calling.

"Today Is a Happy and Blessed Day for St. Francis Parish"
No Date

. . . You could search far and wide in this world without finding a vision quite so noble or quite so ennobling as that of Christ's priesthood. And the reason is that this vision is the very vision of Christ himself. The priest is a priest because he is consecrated and committed to be what Christ *is*, to do what Christ *did*. The priest, more than anything else, is another Christ.

Christ, Our Lord, as you know, came into a world that was separated from God and buried in the worst kind of ignorance and sin. What the world needed more than anything else was someone who could lift the barrier of sin and span the ever-widening gap between God and men. Christ was the perfect go-between, since he was both perfect God and perfect man. A perfect union of God and man that was accomplished in his very person. He came thus prepared, to bring all other men back to God. This was his priestly mission: to bring God to men and men to God.

You recall how he was greeted at the beginning of his public life—behold the Lamb of God, behold him who taketh away the sins of the world. But not only did he come to remove a barrier. He was also to set up a new pattern of living, a new way of life. "I have come that you may have Life and have it more abundantly." "I am the Way, the Truth and the Life." This was the fullness of the gift of Christ, the new and perfect priest: a way of life that those who had been stumbling about in the darkness of error; a new life to those who had long been dead in sins. You know from the Gospel how his three short years of work were committed to this task, how he spent long hours with the rich and poor, the layers, bankers, farmers, workers, fishermen, and housewives—bringing them closer to God and bringing God closer to them.

You can understand how eventually he gave his own life that all of us might live, and how this priestly offering was consummated on Calvary.

All this was not to end with the death of Christ—for there were still millions of souls to be saved, and centuries yet to feel the need of his way and truth and life. So he said to a handful of men: "Receive ye the Holy Spirit. As the Father has sent Me, I send you. Go teach all Nations, commanding them to observe all the things I have taught you, baptizing them in the Name of the Father and of the Son and of the Holy Spirit. Who hears you, hears Me. Whose sins you shall forgive, they are forgiven them." And because Christ gave those first priests the fullness of his priestly mission and powers, he even gave them power over himself, that he might be with his priests and people on all days to strengthen, guide, comfort, and save them. That is why the central part of our celebration here this morning is not my words, or the reception that follows, but the sacred act by which Fr. Van Wolvlear exercises his newly given priestly power to speak in the name of Christ and to renew the priestly mystery, Christ's eternal sacrifice on Calvary, to bring God again into our midst as our Savior and Lord. No wonder that we bow our heads at his words of consecration—for here is a power that not even the Blessed Virgin Mary nor the angels have. Here is the priestly power of Christ vested in one of your own young men. Here is the fulfillment of the words of Holy Scripture, "A priest is taken from among men and consecrated to the things that pertain to God." Here is the vision of God's priesthood that has ever inspired young men to walk in the footsteps of Christ and to respond gladly to his call: "Come, follow Me."

What other words can fill the heart of our new priest today, than the joyful words that Our Blessed Mother uttered at the thought of bringing Christ into a world that so badly needed him: "My soul doth magnify the Lord, and my Spirit has rejoiced in God my savior. . . . For He that is mighty has done great things for me and holy is His name."

The vision that has come to fruition is not ending today but rather beginning. Henceforth Fr. Van Wolvlear can spend himself as Christ spent himself to bring the blessings of God to men and the strivings of men to God. Henceforth, this is his life: To be close to God and close to God's people, to be their means of coming close to God, to be a Christlike go-between as he sacrifices and teaches at the altar, as he forgives their sins in the confessional, as he consoles and guides and saves through life and at the hour of death, to give and give and give with all the priestly powers he has received from Christ, until the shadows lengthen, and his own day is done and the time comes to go home to the Great High Priest with his hands full of the souls he has saved in Christ's name along the highways and byways of this world. Then he too will truly understand what a tremendous grace it is to be a priest of God. Then also we will realize what a great cause we have had for rejoicing today, as he begins his priestly ministrations.

Address at the Annual Convention of the National Federation of Priests' Councils
Baltimore, Maryland, March 15, 1971

Dear fellow priests:

I come to you today with a minimum of official credentials. I am not even a Monsignor, thank God, and *salva reverentia*. My proudest boast is that for the better part of the past twenty-eight years I have been a practicing priest, one who loves to celebrate Mass every day as the greatest act of priesthood for the salvation of the whole world. I have celebrated Mass in all the holy places—St. Peter's, the catacombs, Lourdes, Fatima, Canterbury, Westminster, Geneva, Istanbul, Athens, Jerusalem, and all the rest. But I have perhaps taken greater pleasure celebrating Mass at the University of Moscow, on the operating table at the South Pole, on the campus of a host of secular universities, in scores of humble missions in Asia, Africa, South America, and Australia.

Wherever Mass was offered, it was for everywhere and everybody, with the kind of divine largesse that made me feel very humble and yet very important because I was doing what I loved to do and what was, all the same, very important to be done, far beyond my human capabilities, answering my wildest dreams. In a way, it made up for what seemed lacking in the direct and satisfying work of more personal pastoral contributions to the salvation of the world. I loved the offering so much that I have only missed offering once in all these years—because of a night in a hospital—and while I may have stretched the rules at times, I have always felt in rhythm with the prophecy of Malachi: "From the rising of the sun to the going down thereof, there will be offered among the gentiles a clean oblation," or in the words of the new Canon: "From age to age You gather a people to Yourself, so that from East to West, a perfect oblation may be made to the glory of Your name—to advance the peace and salvation of all the world."

I admit to you that my life has truly been spent among the Gentiles. I keep hoping that, like St. Paul, my ideal patron, it has been the life of an apostle to the Gentiles. Also like St. Paul, I am embarrassed to speak so frankly of myself, but I trust that the good Lord will forgive me since so many other priests today are speaking so frankly of their distaste for the priesthood and their reasons for leaving the priesthood for presumably greener pastures or better identities.

So often they speak of an identity crisis, an ambiguous role as priests, a crushing weight of loneliness, a need for human love, a feeling of uselessness. At the risk of appearing square, simplistic, insensitive, or out-of-touch, may I confess that I have never felt any of these disabilities. Maybe my life has been untypical, but, if so, it has been untypical in that, for much of it, my companions and surroundings have been largely secular, non-Catholic, pagan, and public. I have spent as many nights in hotels as in the monastery, prayed my Breviary more often on airplanes than in the chapel, and have spent a large proportion of my days wrestling with secular problems like the peaceful uses of atomic energy and science generally; civil rights in the fields of voting, education, employment, housing, public accommodations, and the administration of justice; international educational and cultural exchange; space exploration; human development around the world through economic programs and the Peace Corps; university development and food programs; urban studies; volunteer Armed Forces instead of the draft; and a whole host of other largely secular endeavors.

There have been all too few excursions into fields more congenial to my priesthood in the classical sense, like Christian higher education at Notre Dame and around the world, my main task; ecumenism in a Christian and world religion context; renewal and *aggiornamento* in a wide Christian setting; theology pursued almost surreptitiously in odd moments as my first love. But, in large measure, my life has been lived among the Gentiles, largely in gentile endeavors, but with apostolic overtones. Strangely, I have known more popes and cardinals than bishops and archbishops, whatever this might mean. Part of the strange life I have lived perhaps. I could just as well say I've known presidents and senators better than governors or mayors. This is not said to indicate anything other than that if it is possible to live such a life among the Gentiles, even the top Gentiles, and still practice and cherish the ideal of priesthood, it should be possible to practice and cherish it among Catholics in the closer Christian community of parishes and neighborhoods.

Maybe that is a monumental non sequitur, but I do still love to preach and counsel, to baptize and officiate at marriages, to console, absolve, and instruct whenever the occasion permits or invites me to do so.

These opportunities occur less frequently "on the road" than they do in parishes, but if one is always a priest, they do occur and they do brighten each day, whenever they do occur. I might say parenthetically that many of these priestly opportunities would not have occurred if I had not been dressed so as to be discernible as a priest.

I have turned down high government positions and high Church offices when I believed that they might interfere with my being a good priest. I admit this with no special modesty or humility since my overriding concern in each case was not to diminish that which I, perhaps selfishly, cherished most: the freedom to be an apostle to the Gentiles, a priest where no other priest could normally be, a Christian presence where one was generally absent, and not to compromise myself or my priesthood in the process.

I should just as frankly confess that many others could have performed much better than I in these various apostolates— because others are more learned, certainly holier, more capable in many ways. But all of us are what we are, and we must do what we have, for some providential reasons, the opportunity of doing. If we can only open a few doors, lower a few barriers, dissolve a few misunderstandings and prejudices, others more capable or more apostolic will certainly follow in our wake, however messy it might be, and make greater contributions to the kingdom of God among men.

Having said all of this by way of commentary on my lack of official credentials to address you, may I suggest that at least the kind of life I have lived does give me a special kind of perspective on the Church and the world today and the role of the priesthood in both the modern Church and the modern world.

Lest I seem too taken up with modernity, may I say that I am fully in agreement with the wonderful biblical and traditional perceptions of the priesthood outlined in Raymond Brown's recent booklet on *Priest and Bishop* (Paulist Press, 1970). He shows both the richness and the difficulty of the priesthood today, which must encompass the functions of an Old Testament priest, prophet, and scribe. Our priesthood must encompass as well the New Testament notions of disciple, apostle, and minister of the sacrifice and sacrament.

As *disciples*, we must in our total lifestyle both follow and portray Jesus Christ whose unique priesthood we share, by permanent, full-time commitment, by our special vocation which demands more of us than other Christians, by celibacy for the sake of Christ and in total service to Christians as a witness existing almost alone in Roman Catholicism today among the many Christian Communions. As Raymond Brown puts it:

> As one reflects on the challenges offered to the priesthood by the NT portrait of discipleship, one cannot but judge that these ideals have often been poorly met. If our present crisis about the priesthood underlines this, it will have been worth all the anguish. However, it is permissible to wonder whether we are now engaged in simply another of the priestly reform movements that have brought the Gospel ideals to the fore over and over again. To some, at least, it seems that more is being questioned than the success with which priests meet the ideals and that the ideals themselves are being doubted. In other words, the name of the game may be the relevancy of the Gospels—does a 1st-century ideal of discipleship have anything to say to a 20th-century man? I, for one, think that the Gospel challenge to discipleship is just as relevant today as it was in the 1st century because it touches on the very essence of the generosity demanded of men if they are to be open to God's rule or kingdom. If some of the Gospel demands, such as permanent commitment, seem very difficult to us today, I find no proof that they were not very difficult in the 1st century. Others may disagree about the continuing relevance of the specific Gospel ideals of discipleship. So be it my main goal is to try to clarify what values are at stake.

The New Testament concept of *apostle* demands of the priest that he be first a servant of Jesus Christ and then a servant to all his people—who are all people—by the special services of hard work of all kinds, prayer, suffering, correction, and even raising money for good causes—something I loathe, though St. Paul's epistles are full of it. In the modern context, we are especially poor at prayer for and with God's people, and alone. We are poor, too, at courageous correction of ourselves and God's people, even when the fullness of the Christian message in faith and morals, when the complete acceptance of God's Word, in both public and private life, are at stake. It is easier to be popular than prophetic, more convenient to be with it than against it, "it" being the latest current trend. We are likewise poor at the service of suffering, although as apostles we serve the "suffering servant" of Isaiah. Each priest has his own suffering to bear: loneliness for some, misunderstanding or even abuse for others; for some, human inadequacy in the face of enormous human challenges, even difficult with God's own help; for others, the unsettling need to rethink one's specific service, not to be shaken by the departure of dear friends from the priesthood, not to be discouraged when so much effort seems to bear so little fruit. But all of this is redemptive, part of our service of suffering as priests.

Lastly, we are *ministers* of the altar and the sacraments, ministers who must, in the words of our ordination: "understand what we do; imitate what we handle." It all comes down to a daily following and a daily professing and a daily commitment to Jesus Christ and his priesthood. At our best, we will be poor servants, but again as Raymond Brown says in face of a priesthood comprising so much grandeur and so much weakness: "On a deeper level I would think that the only identity crisis truly worthy of the name (for a priest) occurs when, amidst the legitimate differences in priestly work, the priest begins to forget that it is Jesus Christ to whom he is bearing witness. Whatever other claim he may make about what he does, in order to know who he is, a priest must be able to join with Paul in issuing the challenge, 'Become imitators of me as I am of Christ'" (Brown, 45).

This priesthood of ours, so enriched in content and meaning over the years, is confronted today with a situation that requires even more understanding, commitment, and enrichment. Part of our present problem is the enormous change and rate of change in both the Church and the world. Another complicating factor today is the different understanding of the relationship between the temporal (I greatly dislike the usual word, profane) and the sacred. Personally, I believe that the new understanding of the relationship between the temporal and the sacred, an understanding more Eastern than Western, is much more meaningful than the older schizoid notion for an appreciation that every human activity may be both priestly and sanctified, as well as sanctifying. The new notion, which avoids the usual artificial dichotomy between the natural and supernatural, temporal and sacred, follows the Eastern tradition that everything human was sanctified at the moment of Christ's conception, that nothing human or natural is profane once the Word was made flesh and the divine entered human history to elevate and sanctify and make redemptive all that is human and natural. What does this have to say to the world today, with all its hopes, anguishes, and challenges? At the very least, it says that there can be a priestly response to every human hope, anguish, and challenge.

It takes a lot of presuming to presume to give a priestly assessment of the Church and the world today. May I brashly begin by eliminating some of the common causes of dissension and frustration. I realize that one cannot simply eliminate them verbally, but again this is just my own personal assessment of the value or worthlessness of these particular and popular problems. I claim no special wisdom, only the insights that come from one priest's experiences and convictions.

First, the pope, or as I would prefer to call him, our Holy Father. I speak of him in friendship and love that I wish all of you could share. Like each of us, he has his own personality, his own graces—quite special in his case—his own hopes and fears for the kingdom of God on earth, his own educational background, categories of thought, inner lights, and instinctive impressions. From all the world, he was picked for the task he has, by the action of the Holy Spirit, I believe, and has assumed one of the most difficult of all tasks because of the times in which we live today. I am sure that each day, under enormous pressures unknown to us, he does the very best he can—as each of us would, were we in his place. His infallibility is limited indeed, however you view it theologically. His anguish and suffering must be great, considering the magnitude of his daily problems and the paucity of really efficacious answers in a world of real and pervasive evil.

With the bark of Peter rocking from side to side as never before, somehow he has to keep it moving forward toward its eternal goal, which is also ours. One need not believe that his performance is perfect, nor would ours be perfect were we in his place. We can be Christianly critical at times, but equally loyal and understanding when we view the magnitude of his task and the limitations of his humanity, even granting his special divine guidance. Again, my response is simple, but I trust loyal and friendly: I remember him first of all at the Offertory of my Mass each day, for all the light and strength he needs. And, when I disagree with him, I do so privately and honestly and with affection.

Lest I seem too simplistic, may I say that it is possible to criticize the system, for example the Curia, without by that action criticizing our Holy Father. And, while on this subject, may I say that Pope Paul VI has more radically changed the system of the Curia than any dozen of his predecessors since the Curia began. One recent action of his accomplished what our own Congress does not have the courage or wisdom to do, namely place an age limit that totally changes the leverage of decision and election in the Church.

You may say that some other pope might have done more. I only say that all the others in recent history have done less. Also, there will still be others, with their special graces and charisma, but each Holy Father must be himself and we must believe that the Holy Spirit will guide both the election and action of each Holy Father in each successive age of the Church's long history through darkness into light.

Then there is the hierarchy, another great cause of contention in today's Church. I suppose that all of us are somewhat unhappy today about the technicalities and criteria that govern the selection of bishops. Everything seems to lead to the selection of men who are safe, uncontroversial, favorably disposed to Rome and preferably Roman-educated, seminary rectors or canon lawyers or episcopal secretaries, in a word, generally those who will not make waves.

It is objected that a majority of such men will give us a bland leadership in a Church that was founded to cast fire on the earth. Put in the opposite focus, it will assure that those priests who have manifested dynamic leadership, who, therefore, are controversial or liberal, or especially intellectual and committed to a broader sense of academic freedom, stand almost no chance of ever assuming leadership in a Church that is led by those chosen to be bishops.

This is, of course, an oversimplification which, unfortunately, is more true than false. However, there are those who were selected because of their pastoral concern, which is safe, if spiritual, and not too enmeshed in the controversial problems of the day. There are also those who almost by mistake get appointed and then disappointed if they act against the system and incur the displeasure of the powerful within the hierarchy.

What is the solution to this problem? You and I know the answers that have been unavailingly offered: Choice of bishops by the priests and people of a diocese according to a more ancient Christian pattern that gave us, for example, St. Ambrose. Of course, this method is not infallible either and could degenerate into a popularity contest which generally delivers mediocrity rather than a person demanding quality. However, this is

self-corrective after people are made to live with their own bad
choices, as we do in the democratic political process. At least,
such a method of more popular choice, under the guidance of
the Holy Spirit, would avoid the horrible human anomaly that
exists in some dioceses in the world today where the vast majority of the priests and people simply reject the ecclesiastical leader
imposed upon them by the system. How can a bishop possibly
lead those who seriously reject him for very serious and very
Christian reasons?

One might say that in a monarchical system, priests and
laymen have no other choice, but a simple reading of the Gospel, the Epistles, and the Acts of the Apostles would convince
any reader that such a monarchical system, at least in its worst
aspects, is hardly essential to the good news of salvation as proclaimed by our humble Savior and as practiced in the early centuries of the Church.

If one were to err today in any direction, it would seem to me
that the system less open to error is to let the Holy Spirit inspire
those most concerned in the local Church to choose their own
leadership on the basis of the charismatic qualities displayed by
the most outstanding local Christians. St. Anselm was chosen as
a layman, and did quite well after being consecrated Archbishop
of Milan.

A knowledgeable cleric told me the other day that he was
happy about what he called the undistinguished quality of the
American hierarchy because this made it easier for leadership
to come from other sources in the Church. I am not sure that
I agree with him. In the early Church of St. Paul, Corinth may
have been able to get along without a bishop, with considerable prodding from St. Paul, but we happen to be a hierarchical
Church and, given that fact, however it has developed under the
impetus of Our Lord and the Holy Spirit, it seems to me that we
had better do everything possible to get great leaders as bishops.
If the present system of selection is not working, then we had

better put our greatest efforts into the inauguration of a different and better system.

In the meanwhile, we had better not expect great theological leadership from those bishops who are not theologians, or great social leadership from those persons who showed no signs of great social leadership before becoming bishops. Other resources in the Church can provide this, laymen and priests, and they should. The Holy Spirit will not fail us. Let us also admit at this point that there are few positions in the world today less envious and more troublesome than that of the bishop, with the possible exception of the university president. At least, presidents may quit, as many of them have, but the bishop must endure until age seventy-five before being provided this escape. Here, too, there might be more flexibility. University presidents quit because they feel they are no longer acceptable to their constituency and, therefore, disqualified as leaders of that constituency. Should bishops feel less free? They, like us priests, are married to the Church, but not necessarily to a particular role in a particular place which can become impossible of true accomplishment in very troubled times.

After all, St. Paul lived his whole apostolic life without ever becoming the bishop of a particular community. If there were more possibilities of functional rather than residential bishoprics, we might solve many problems. At least, this is done for the military, although there are specialized needs and problems just as urgent among other classes of Christians—such as university faculties and students, youth generally, professional people such as lawyers and doctors, and others such as the inner city and rural poor. All of these need specialized attention, represent a functionally different apostolate, and number, as individual groups, far more people than the military—which now alone has its specialized bishops and priests.

We should not get hung up about a hierarchy that argues for hours, and by the gimmick of a two-thirds vote that thwarts the will of the majority, for a method of Holy Communion described and accepted in the *Didache*, the earliest description of the practice of the early Christian community after the New Testament, which is fairly silent on the subject. Rather than griping about this, we should insist that there are far greater problems facing the Christian community at the moment and we should press for Christian answers to them: war and peace; racial justice; the realistic recognition of and contribution to human dignity and human development across the world; the human and humane uses of science and technology; the responsibilities of wealthy and affluent nations and people; the sanctity of human life as abused by a growing cult and legalization of abortion; Christian liberty and the draft for military service; Christian conscience and its obligations; Christian education and a better understanding of the young who, if lost, signalize the loss of untold millions in succeeding generations.

We were told in the recent Koval [John M.] study that the main reason for one out of four Catholic priests in America considering leaving the priesthood is their disillusionment with the leadership of those in authority in the Church.

I would say to them, and to all of you, that if our perception of the priesthood of Christ is as shallow as this, we should never have been ordained priests in the first place. We are priests of Christ, not of the hierarchy; we are committed to the apostolate of Christ, our best leader, and if we do not get leadership from our other leaders, we can pray to the Holy Spirit to get it from him, together with the courage to exercise personal leadership on our own level, whatever the cost to our personal feelings, convenience, or ambition.

Military and political history is filled with examples of inept generals and kings with brilliant lieutenants and governors who carried the day despite them, and they did not have the promise of the Holy Spirit for all days as we have. At the risk of seeming insensitive, may I say that the priest who quits because of the lack of leadership is himself a non-leader, which no priest should be.

He who quits because Vatican II is not coming into reality quickly enough simply admits that he lacks the subsidiary leadership and imagination to make it come to pass in the little world of his own activity. In a word, he is blaming others for his own lack of dedication to the Holy Spirit, the Spirit of truth, love, courage, and vision. And if, as the same Koval survey tells us, half of the priests under thirty are wavering because of their "desire to marry," let them marry and leave to a small, but totally dedicated remnant, the main and central work of the kingdom of God. There are many things that I do not know, but I do know this: that celibacy is important to the totally dedicated apostolate, even though there may be less totally dedicated apostolates in the Church. I also know this—that one must say "yes" or "no" to celibacy—but never "maybe." He who says "maybe" has already conceded the day. Unfortunately, too many of the younger clergy are not saying "yes" or "no," but "maybe." There must be a better term for them than optional celibacy—like optional salad or optional power steering—a better ideal than "maybe yes," "maybe no" to the question of total dedication.

This will seem unduly harsh, and I speak from the lifelong perspective of a priest who is also a member of a religious community, but the present crisis is such that we will not be able to do what must be done if we cannot count on total dedication in the evangelical tradition for some numbers of priests, both religious and diocesan. I do not discount the possible contribution of married priests, particularly in certain areas of contemporary life, but they will not be the shock troops that will carry the day against the monumental powers of darkness that presently threaten the People of God. If I must call a spade a spade in the matter of the hierarchy, I should be equally honest in speaking to my fellow priests. We have indulged ourselves in too much nonsense which has cheapened both ourselves and our perception of our priesthood.

I would remind you that the Hindu Gandhi, when faced with the monumental problem of liberating India from colonialism, vowed and observed celibacy for the last twenty-five years of his life, even though he was married. The fact that millions of Hindus followed him as their spiritual leader was not unrelated to this symbolism of his total dedication to the cause. Does our cause call for less dedication?

It is often alleged today that we are suffering in the Church a crisis of authority or a crisis of leadership. Wrong on both counts. What we are really suffering is *a crisis of vision*. It is the vision of Christ and his good news, his salvific message, that vivifies the Christian community, age after age, and gives new life and continual inspiration to every priest in every age. It is the lack of this vision, as it applies to any particular age, that stultifies the Christian community, that deprives it of leadership, or degrades the exercise of authority within it, and empties the priesthood of its splendor. And we are all most fundamentally priests, the Holy Father, the cardinals, archbishops, bishops, and all of us.

After years of a codified, formalized, and desiccated Christianity, that allowed and suffered every form of social injustice and un-charity—I spare you the details—Vatican II gave us a new and truly evangelical charter. You may say it was inchoate, incomplete, and even embryonic. But it was a breath of fresh air in a stale scene, a new vision of Christlike splendor that we, and the world, badly needed. It came fundamentally because of the vision of a man called John, and it was committed to a man called Paul. This new charter was also committed to all and each of us, to every Christian.

The Pilgrim Church is still on its pilgrim way, as we pray in the Canon of the Mass each day that it may be strengthened in faith and love. We still have trouble shucking off the dead trappings of a past triumphalistic way, all the false and fastidious trappings of a dead monarchical past, but at least, thanks to Vatican II, a beginning has been made. We have seen more change for constructive good in the Church during the past ten years than during the past four hundred. We are on the way. This is not time to lose heart, or to leave the Church in its most exciting and exhilarating period in centuries. We may not generally have superb leadership or may not even give great leadership ourselves, but there are some superb leaders in our midst. Let us follow them and the lead of the Holy Spirit who inspires them and, hopefully, us too.

I should say at this point that no hierarchy in the world has a better or more forthright and courageous leader than John Cardinal Dearden. Baltimore's Archbishop, Lawrence Cardinal Shehan, was the first pastor I worked for in Washington as a newly ordained priest. No one could have been more helpful, more understanding, more compassionate to a young and inexperienced priest than he was, and he has, in his recent nighttime visit to his jailed priests, showed the same compassion and understanding that I enjoyed and needed twenty-eight years ago in St. Patrick's Parish on 10th and G Streets in Washington. There are other bishops, too, who have known and understood the good yearnings of this association and its members. May the Holy Spirit increase their number and our fidelity to the Church's high mission, the vision we share with them.

This leads me to my final observation. The important question before the house today is not the purpose or effectiveness of your organization or the frustration of your membership. It is the kingdom of God and the condition of the People of God that is important. This transcends your federation, your personal problems, even your ecclesiastical leaders. The present and future spiritual status of the kingdom of God and the People of God in our country and in our times is the concern of our priesthood, that we share with our Holy Father and our bishops. It is the most important reality in our lives and theirs. Only the priesthood can put the problems and the opportunities in hopeful and promising Christian focus.

I spoke earlier of the Church and the world and, in doing so, I was not envisioning two great organizations, but two great realities that must interact upon each other. Looking upon the world today, with all its injustices, inequities, and moral ambiguities, one might very well be pessimistic. But when one considers the possible salvific influence of the Church in the world, one begins to hope that things might be different. The difference is in our personal exercise of priesthood. No ambiguity or lack of goal or role here; no task so unimportant that loneliness puts us off; no lack of vision if we will prayerfully seek it from the Holy Spirit who has been promised to us; no discouragement or frustration if we really know what priesthood means: to mediate between what is and what might be with the grace of God; to stand between the hope of salvation and the despair of damnation, to uphold the ideal, even though the real is dismal; to work and sacrifice and pray and not to despair or give up—because the good news has been announced long ago by the good Lord and we in this day have the great and noble task of proclaiming it anew. May we do so with the courage of Christ and the inspiration of the Holy Spirit and in keeping with the splendor of his vision, whatever our weakness or the magnitude of the challenges that face us. However few we are, let us remember that it all began with twelve apostles, one of whom left, and a totally pagan world. The odds are much less today, and the same Holy Spirit is still with us.

Reflections on Priesthood
Darlington, Maryland, September 11, 1983

It has been suggested that I speak today of priesthood, since I celebrated last June my fortieth anniversary of ordination. If you will forgive me some personal observations, I would be glad to reflect with you on this subject.

My first word must be one of thanksgiving to the good Lord and priest, Jesus, and His Mother, who is also the mother of all priests. She has to be closer to the reality of priesthood than any other human being, since she brought the Savior into the world and gave Him for all in sacrifice. For Her motherly care, to which I commend all of you, I am indeed grateful.

I never wanted to be anything but a priest, which is in itself a great and unearned grace. I hope to live and die a priest, nothing more, but nothing less either. I would not trade my priesthood for any other position one might imagine, not the power of the US presidency, not the millions of the wealthiest, not the fantasies that anyone might imagine.

In a simple way, I best imagine the priestly role as one of mediation. The priest stands between God and humankind and brings the blessing and graces of God to humans while also, in the other direction, bringing their hopes and needs and desires to God, hopefully, bringing them to God, too, by praying with and for them all, by trying to inspire them by God's words in faith, hope, and charity, which virtues also bring them to God.

The priest is a man in the middle and, as a mediator, he bridges the gap between the human and the divine, between time and eternity. To be a good mediator, he has to be close to both God and humans. None of us are ever as close as we ought to be to God, even though He is always close to us. Our prayer reflects this all too little and too seldom for which we can only say *mea culpa* and try harder to be more conscious of the all-pervading presence of God, especially to His priests who are in a very real sense His ambassadors on earth. We are not here to present ourselves, but Him.

It is much easier to be closer to humans. We see them; we are always with them; it requires no deep abiding faith to sense their presence and their needs, as it does to sense the abiding presence of God and our deep need for grace.

The good Lord has made all this easier for us by telling us that when we do something needful for others, especially our least brothers and sisters, we are loving and serving Him in them. It still is the easiest way of finding Him and serving Him in those who are spiritually and materially hungry and thirsty, naked and homeless, sick and in prison.

I do not want to make it sound too easy because the least brothers and sisters are not the most attractive humans we meet. They are often old and smelly, ugly and uncaring, twisted and ungrateful. How much easier to mediate God and His blessings to attractive, successful, caring, fun-filled young men and women. Besides, they respect us, love us, lionize us, and massage our egos. Well, a priest has some of each, but must take care that the poor, the powerless, the outcast, and the lost souls get his prime attention whenever possible. They need God most of all and we need to find and serve God in them most of all.

The greatest priestly act of mediation is, of course, the Mass. There is really only one true priest and mediator, Christ the God-man, *fans et origo totius sacerdotii*, the fount and origin of all priesthood, as St. Thomas put it, and it is His one eternal human-divine sacrifice at Calvary that bridged the total chasm of all past, present, and future human evil, called sin, and made it possible for all of us to possess God and His eternal life.

Our greatest privilege is to share His priesthood and to renew His sacrifice daily for our people and our age. When you stand at the altar and hold wide your arms in supplication, you are embracing the whole world, East and West, North and South, men, women, and children, good and evil, Christian and non-Christian, believers and unbelievers. The Eternal Priest died for all of them and we show forth His death and His gift for all every time we offer Mass.

If you will excuse the personal allusion, I cite it only to make the point, I have only missed offering Mass one day in my priestly life during all the days, except Good Friday, when Mass is possible. This is not to brag, but to thank God for the greatest priestly possibility. I remember offering Mass at the South Pole, at the Faculty House at the University of Moscow, at great cities like Chung-du, Taskent, and Sammerkand where millions live their lives with never a Mass in their midst. At least that day they were all remembered in a special way.

I think of the Mass offered in times of great sorrow and great joy, at funerals and marriages, in the midst of war and violence—and in the peace of Christian families at home. It is always the greatest and the best that a priest can offer God Himself for the salvation of the world. I have been greedy to exercise this great privilege and you should be, too. Nothing else we do will be more priestly.

We have so many other wonderful priestly ways of mediating grace which is to say giving divine life. I love baptisms, infants certainly, but adults even more. Confirmation now and then is a special joy because I wrote my theological thesis on it and believe so deeply in the apostolate of the laity in the Church, for which confirmation qualifies and deputes them.

Care of the dying is a special grace for us when we boost the worried soul into eternity in peace. Confessions are fewer today, but I would say better, more soul-searching and less routine. They also call for more priestly counsel and that, too, is good for us, as well as them. I used to think before first hearing confessions that I would be disillusioned with fellow human beings. Quite the opposite. I soon learned that they were inspiring me by their honesty and humility. I have never spoken a harsh word to any penitent and never will. One of the greatest joys of priesthood is to mediate the compassion, the understanding, and the eternal forgiveness of God, especially since we all need it so much ourselves.

Preaching the Word of God is another joy, but we preach it badly if we do not meditate on it often. The Word of God has its own power and light. Again we are mediating this power and light of Christ, not creating it. I confess to liking John's Gospel best of all because of his recurring emphasis on the trilogy of light, life, and love. I also try to read St. Paul's letters on retreat each year. Somehow, the current theological controversies about Christology seem a bit shallow and shrill alongside the strong words of Paul whenever he speaks so personally of Christ whose Apostle he is in every time and place. No attachment is more important for a priest who is quintessentially an apostle. "Who will separate us from the love of Christ," Paul asks. If it ever occurs, this separation, the heart has gone out of our priesthood.

With Christ, the priest has all he needs, all the courage, all the love, all the fidelity, all the compassion, all the consecration, all the faith and hope, all the perseverance. Not that any of us have anything eternally valuable in and of ourselves, to make us dare to share Christ's priesthood, but with Him as our nearest companion and friend, all will go well, despite our weaknesses, inadequacies, faults, and sins.

In my forty years of priesthood, I have successively spent two years in advanced study of theology, four years teaching and thirty-four years in administrative posts. I probably have spent much more time with non-Catholics than Catholics when away from Notre Dame on public and private assignments. The work has been mostly secular, but always with a spiritual and moral dimension, days on end hundreds or thousands of miles away from the nearest church, thousands and thousands of casual encounters with strangers passing like ships in the night, and yet through the millions of miles and more than a hundred countries, I never felt less than a priest. The days and nights were almost always too busy, the claims on my time next to impossible, and yet there was always time for Mass and Breviary, rosary and other daily prayers, never enough for lengthy meditation, probably my fault.

Three religious vows were essential to such a life, at least in my case. Poverty was a great relief, not to have material worries, especially for myself. Enough for living, nothing for amassing, simplicity rather than fine-tuned concerns about room, clothes, cars, or luxuries. The key to poverty is not so much being poor— my life has been far from that—but being unattached to material things that concern most people so much. Freedom of spirit is of the essence of the spirit of poverty. As a priest, freedom is essential. You cannot ever be bought or chained down by possessions.

Chastity or celibacy is another strength of a priest, if he understands it as belonging to no one human so he can belong to and serve all. If we belong to no one so we need not be bothered and can live a life of our own convenience, then we are simply selfish bachelors. Chastity is no big deal if one works at it daily, not fearfully, but resolutely, believing in the commitment we made for one reason only: to give ourselves more fully to Him and His people in priesthood. Without this, I would never make the commitment to celibacy. But as an adjunct to a giving, loving priestly life, celibacy is a great strength and indeed a fulfillment —because of so many thousands of wonderful people, young and old, men and women, who instinctively call you "Father" and mean it.

Obedience is probably the hardest commitment of all because we are all so wedded to our own desires, especially as to where we will live and where we will work. I was asked three times in the first ten years after Ordination what I preferred to do. Each time I expressed my preference and was given another quite different assignment. It did not maim or kill me. As an old Jesuit friend of mine once said, "Success in life is getting what you want and happiness is wanting what you get." I can only say, try to do the best you can to contribute as a priest whenever and wherever need is indicated and you are assigned. You will be at peace and happier, too.

I realize that I have just been speaking about the religious vows and you are becoming diocesan priests. Even so, you will pledge celibacy, practice the poverty of detachment, and obey when the call comes—if you want to be a good priest. Speaking of that, a great priest friend of mine, Jack Egan of Chicago, asked a Jewish social organizer, Saul Alinsky, for his advice on being a good priest. Saul said, "You just said it, just work at being a good priest and don't worry about becoming a Monsignor, a Bishop or Archbishop, or Cardinal." Clerical ambition has ruined many a great young priest.

I have one given in religious life—community—which somehow you will have to provide for. It is very important to maintain a circle of friends who are like-minded and like-committed.
Other friends will help, mainly by what they expect of you. A
great percentage of my oldest and best lay friends—because of
the particular life I have led—are not Catholic, some not even
believers. But they all respect deeply what I am as a priest and
they expect more of me—even as a friend. I must say they give
more, too, maybe they think I need it, which may explain why
we are such good friends. Many of them are women, too. In
some ways, I think they actually feel less inhibited with me
because they instinctively understand and appreciate celibacy
the fact that by choice we priests are out of circulation. This can,
of course, all be a pitfall, but so can almost everything in life—
money, pleasure, power, position if one is not honest with oneself
and one's commitment. Incidentally, and parenthetically, I have
always found it enormously helpful to wear clerical garb when
in public. It also attracts a lot of priestly business that otherwise
would be missed.

Perhaps my university habitat is showing, but I must insist
that there is at least a presumption that as a professional man
one in service to others a priest will remain intellectually alive
by reading good books and having some hobbies more intelligent than cribbage or golf—even though he needs his normal
recreation and exercise, too. Too many priests, and other pro-
fessionals, simply go to seed after a fine education. They thereby
become less competent, less informed, less alive, yes, less attractive, too—all of which makes us less apostolic.

By now, I am sure you will agree that I have done enough
ruminating—maybe too much. I wish you all the love, all the
joy, all the inspiration, all the excitement, all the fulfillment that
I have had, as a priest, through no great virtue of my own, I must
add. It has been all I expected as a priest, and much more. I am
sure that with greater effort on my part, I would have been a
better priest, but as Paul says, "By the grace of God, I am what I

am." I am glad I am a priest, and you should thank God if He is calling you to share His priesthood.

One final word, perhaps the most important of all. Given the sweep of the priestly mission, to be and to act as Christ Himself in the difficult secular, hedonistic, unspiritual world of today, is it not a bit preposterous that any person really aspires to being a priest? The answer is simply, yes, it is preposterous, if you think you can make it on your own. But our Master said He was not going to leave us orphans, alone. First, He said He would be with us all days, but particularly, He said that He was sending us the Holy Spirit who would tell us what to say and what to do. Was it not preposterous to send twelve fearful and ignorant men, one a traitor as well, out to save and redeem a world as bad as ours—in fact, probably worse. They never would have made it without the transformation of Pentecost. I pity any man, however talented, endowed, intelligent, even handsome, who tries to be a priest today without constantly saying that simplest and most efficacious of all prayers: "Come Holy Spirit." I can testify that I have seen it change darkness into light, death into life, hatred into love. Those simple three words call upon the promise of Jesus to give us all days the light and strength of His Spirit. With that key to such enormous power, we can really understand what Jesus said to all priests. "In the world you will have difficulty, but do not fear. I have overcome the world." And St. Paul, "I can do all things in Him who strengthens me." Come Holy Spirit. Come Lord Jesus.

LAITY

The Christian Family
Feast of the Holy Family, December 28, 1947

At the end of each year comes the tender heart-warming message of Christmas. The weary world relives again with joy and hope that never-to-be-forgotten day when to us a Child was born, and a Savior given. Each year as young and old kneel at the crib, all feel assured that the Divine Child on the straw has all the answers to the many problems of our plush but often unhappy world.

Now today, before this lovely picture fades into the forgetfulness and promise of a new year, the Church asks all the world to celebrate the Feast of the Holy Family. We are told to widen our gaze for one last look, to take in the silent adoring figures on each side of the manger, the figures of Mary and Joseph. We are reminded that Christ's coming into the stable did not merely make a trio, but a family. Here in these three holiest persons who ever graced our world, we find the prototype and exemplar of every Christian family, yes, of the families you men hope to found some day. Here too in the Holy Family, we find one of the most important answers to the restless seeking of our day for peace, security, and happiness.

It would be difficult to find a more important element in life than the family, for it is in the family that life originates, develops, and fructifies. Yet in our day, there is hardly any other element of society more under fire than the family, and it is not exaggerating to say that the Christian family is fighting for its life.

Consider these figures for a moment. Twenty-five percent of American couples do not have any children at all. It simply isn't fashionable. The next 20 percent have one child only. Twenty percent more have two children, which is not even enough to balance our population. Now these couples, 65 percent of all American couples, are happy and contented in marriage. Again, the figures speak for themselves. Sixty-six percent of our divorces come from couples who have no children, or only one or two children. On the other hand, couples with five children represent less than 1 percent of the divorces granted in this country.

It seems obvious from this actual state of affairs that our big families are our happy families. The reason is that you have to be big yourself to live and grow in a big family. And if you are big yourself, you are kept too busy finding things to do for other people, to have time to find fault with them. A husband and a wife work best together as a father and a mother.

It is a strange thing in our world today which has made so much progress in making life comfortable, has made so little progress in making life livable. It is strange that a country so rich and prosperous as ours has so little use for children who are the greatest riches and prosperity of a country. We spend billions of dollars a year on luxuries, but when it comes to having children, so many say: "We can't afford them." We utilize the best heads of science improving health and lengthening the span of life, but when it comes to bringing life into the world, they devise means of preventing it. We put our best executives to work activating housing projects, but when it comes to making homes of our fine houses, so many people simply renege.

The young married couple who are courageous, who decide to follow God's way instead of the world's way for married life, are met with scorn and often enough eviction. Lest he be bothered again, the landlord placards his door with a sign: "No children and no pets allowed." Think what those horrible words mean. They mean that human babies, the most significant earthly creation of God's love and the love of husband and wife for each other, are put in this same category as cats and dogs. In some classes of society, cats and dogs simply replace them.

To add insult to injury, as soon as the notice of the new birth is listed in the public papers, our efficient modern propaganda machinery goes into high gear. The deluded young couple, for so they seem to the modern mind, are deluged with so-called enlightening but actually filthy literature telling them twenty new ways of practicing birth control. This is the freedom he was fighting for overseas, scarcely a year ago: the freedom for someone in a swank office on Fifth Avenue to insult him through the mail. This is the home she dreamed about while she prayed for his safe return from the war: a single drab and dingy room, with a daybed in one corner, and in another, a portable hot plate instead of a cozy kitchen.

Oh their hearts may well ache, but these courageous young Christian couples of today need not fear. For the hearts of Mary and Joseph must also have ached to see the long awaited of the nations, the Savior of the world turned away from door to door, brought to the light of the world he made in a cold and drafty stable. They too had to face eviction by the cruel and heartless Herod. Theirs too were the hardships of the flight into Egypt.

But if holiness is happiness, well can we wish all the courageous couples of today all the heavenly bliss that filled the hearts of that first Holy Family through all their trials and hardship. With all the coldness of the modern world, at least our couples know that they are not turning away Christ again. They indeed are cradling the Christ Child in the baptized soul of their baby. Theirs too is the consolation of hearing the words of Christ for them: "Whosoever receiveth such a little one in My name, receiveth Me."

The world today may go its way, turning away by the millions babies that could and should be born for the glory of God, but let them not call themselves Christian for it was Christ who said: "Suffer the little ones to come unto Me, for of such is the kingdom of heaven." Heartless modern people who are wedded to the dollar may go on, closing their doors and making life difficult for couples with children, but they too will one day face the Christ who said: "Whatsoever you did unto one of these my least brethren, you did it unto Me."

My dear friends, never forget that God is not mocked. The world may make and break its own rules about marriage, but it cannot find happiness in marriage apart from God and God's way. You can take all the riches and all the luxuries of our childless American houses and add them all together, and still they will not begin to spell out the happiness that filled the hearts of the Holy Family there in the stable. For this is a happiness that comes from God, and from being faithful to his way, a tender and lasting family happiness that is reflected in every Christian family of every age, and which will be reflected also in the family that many of you will found one day, please God.

Family Values and Christian Ethics in the Modern World
No Date

. . . If there is anything in the world that gives Holy Cross priests a greater thrill than a railful of Notre Dame men, it is a world full of Notre Dame families. Maybe a little story will bring out what I mean.

Some years ago, Bishop McNamara of Washington was confirming a group of school children. He was explaining to them the meaning of confirmation: becoming strong and militant Christians—and illustrated it by the example of all the Christian children who died martyrs' deaths for Christ during the Roman persecutions. "Now what are *you* going to do?" he asked the confirmation class. A little boy popped up and said, "We can't die for Christ, but we'll *live* for Christ."

If we are trying to accomplish anything at Notre Dame, it is to train men to live for Christ in the modern world. But life is not lived in a vacuum.

If there is any one factor that looms large in the life of most Notre Dame men, it is their marriage and their family. And if there is any one great need in the modern world, it is the crying need for good Catholic marriages and staunch Catholic families that are based on a Notre Dame way of life.

Maybe the world has missed this angle of Notre Dame—you may remember the article about Notre Dame in *Time* magazine two years ago. They mentioned many of the fine things Notre Dame is trying to do with its men. But they, sharp as they are, missed something. Dan Culhane's wife wrote in one short sentence to the corresponding column, "Dear Sirs—Notre Dame also turns out the finest husbands in the world."

Westbrook Pegler had something to say about Notre Dame men last week too—and I think he too missed the target. We'll all agree that we do want great politicians and great world leaders from Notre Dame but that hardly constitutes the bulk of our mission. We are aiming at an overall greatness that never makes the headlines or the inner circle of the Washington merry-go-round. Let's call it the humble, self-effacing greatness of Christian fatherhood—and, indirectly, the sublime greatness of Christian motherhood—for both forms of greatness go together and are achieved together.

In the long run, what other greatness, in politics, or business, or public life is comparable to this. Suppose, to be fanciful, that Notre Dame did turn out a Shakespeare, a Beethoven, a Washington, or a Lincoln. Their works may captivate the imagination of millions of people—for decades, and even centuries. But the day will come, when their works will pass into the end of time and be no more. Not so with the work of Christian fathers and mothers, for their work is bound up in the giving and training of human life—life that will never end. A million years from today, your work will live on in the lives of your children—for without your marriage, those lives would never have been. Thanks to your marriage—and your consecrated life, together in Christ— God is being glorified in an eternal way that would not have been possible without you men and women of Notre Dame.

What work could be greater than this eternal work—this co-creating of human beings with God—this molding of eternal souls created for his everlasting honor and glory. And what greater greatness is needed in the modern world. A few statistics may clarify this need.

Late in the nineteenth century, America led the world divorce rate with 25,000 annually. By 1947 we had increased that number to 620,000 annually, an overall average of one for every three marriages. In large cities it worked out one for every two. Now how can these be good families without good marriages?

On the other hand, Paul Popenoe of Southern California— lest we forget—has estimated that 25 percent of American wives have no children, 20 percent more have one child, 20 percent more have two children. That means roughly 65 percent of all American wives have no children, one child, or two children at most. Now more than three children per marriage are needed to keep America in Americans.

There is a good statistical tie between these twin American evils of divorce and birth prevention. Nimkoff—a marriage expert from Bucknell University—estimates that 55 percent of divorces are granted to childless couples—22 percent to marriages with one child—9 percent to marriages with two children. In all, over 86 percent of all divorces go to marriages with none, one or two children. So you see it is a vicious circle that bodes no good for our nation—unfruitful marriages generating selfishness and divorces and while conversely the impending shadow of divorce keeps marriages sterile, ungenerous, and unproductive.

. . . Maybe we should adjust our idea of greatness. Should not true greatness diffuse itself upon a world that needs it, in the manner and measure that the world needs it?

Your presence here today—as Notre Dame families—is for us a true measure of greatness. We pray that more and more, Notre Dame may give greatness like yours to the world—the greatness of Christian fatherhood and motherhood, the greatness of staunch Catholic families, the greatness of the spirit of Notre Dame spreading out in so many new lives who will love and lead others to love Notre Dame, Our Mother and her divine Son.

God bless and keep you all.

Teaching Theology to the Layman
No Date

Several weeks ago, when mentioning to a fellow priest that I was having trouble with this paper, he said, "Well, it shouldn't be too difficult. You know what theology is, and what a layman is." That is true. Everybody here knows what theology is, and what a layman is, but like sauerkraut and corned beef, we seldom put them together in our minds. Corned beef calls for cabbage, and theology seems to call for the clergy, not the laity.

After some investigation, however, it seems that, more and more today, theology and the layman are coming into closer contact, or at least there is considerable striving in that direction. Strangely enough, much of the initiative is on the part of the laymen who are seeking out theology and looking to theology for something that is essential to their Catholic life and action.

Less than ten years ago, Étienne Gilson wrote, "Theology alone can teach us what is the ultimate purpose of nature and intelligence, putting before our eyes the truths that God has revealed, truths that enrich with most profound perspectives, those other truths that science teaches. . . ." I would say, he continues, "a man could become a scholar, a philosopher, an artist without having studied theology, but without theology, he could never become a Christian scholar, philosopher or artist. Without it we could well become on the one hand Christians, and on the other, scholars, philosophers or artists, but never without theology, will our Christianity descend into our knowledge, philosophy or art to reform them inwardly and to revivify them."[1]

Gilson then goes on to explain that we here face a new problem. In the Middle Ages the sciences were the privilege of the clerics who also had a good grasp of theology. Their knowledge was thus balanced and well ordered. But today, by reason of a long evolution of secularism, those who follow the sciences do not generally learn theology as a part of their intellectual formation, and most theologians are not well versed in the secular branches of knowledge.

Gilson deplores this secularized state of affairs and affirms that theology must be brought to those who wish to consecrate their intelligence to the cause of Christ the King—in the sciences, in philosophy, in the arts. He says, "to select the basic principles, to organize the teaching, to give it to those whom she judges worthy—that is the work of the teaching Church."[2] But he insists that the laity, the learning Church, can at least make known their needs, as he so eloquently does.

Much more recently than Gilson, just two years ago to be exact, Jacques Maritain said much the same thing at Yale. Speaking to a predominantly non-Catholic audience, Maritain affirms quite fearlessly: "Now those who share the Christian creed know that another rational wisdom, which is rooted in faith, not reason alone, is superior to the merely human wisdom of metaphysics. As a matter of fact, theological problems and controversies have permeated the whole development of Western culture and civilization, and are still at work in its depths, in such a way that the one who would ignore them would be fundamentally unable to grasp his own times and the meaning of its internal conflicts. . . . No one can do without theology, at least a concealed and unconscious theology, and the best way of avoiding the inconveniences of an insinuated theology, is to deal with theology that is consciously aware of itself. Liberal education cannot complete its task without the knowledge of the specific realm and concerns of theological wisdom."

"As a result," he concludes, "a theological course should be given during the last two or three years of study of humanities."[3] And "such teaching should remain thoroughly distinct from the one given in religious seminaries, and should be adapted to the particular needs of laymen; its aim should not be to form a priest, a minister, a rabbi, but to enlighten students of secular matters about the great doctrines and perspectives of theological wisdom."[4]

I have quoted these two great Catholic laymen at some length, because of their high qualifications to speak on this subject, both as intelligent laymen and zealous Christians. Moreover, their words state, rather clearly, the basic issues involved in this question of teaching theology to the layman. Being philosophers, they have resolved the problem into its two ultimate postulates

(1) Why the layman needs theology today, and (2) What kind of theology he needs most today.

This too shall be our order of development.

1. Why Teach Theology to the Layman?

This question is the more speculative of the two, yet it has this practical aspect, that we cannot begin to discuss what procedure should be followed in teaching theology to the layman, unless we are first agreed that there is some reason for teaching him theology at all.

There is no one who has argued more logically and more conclusively for the teaching of theology to the layman than Cardinal Newman. It would be difficult to measure the broad influence of his reasoning in *The Idea of a University*. His argument is basic. He does not appeal to Divine Revelation, Holy Scripture, or the decisions of the Church to support his case. He merely reasons from the notion of what a university purports to be, and what theology is in relation to the function of a university.

Newman develops his point in three logical steps.

First, he establishes the fact that a university is established to teach all sciences, and that theology is one of these sciences to which a university is by its very nature committed. His own words are more conclusive than mine.

> If then, in an institution which professes all knowledge, nothing is professed, nothing is taught about the Supreme Being, it is fair to infer that every individual in the number of those who advocate that Institution, supposing him consistent, distinctly holds that nothing is known for certain about the Supreme Being, nothing such as to have any claim to be regarded as a material addition to the stock of general knowledge existing in the world. If on the other hand, it turns out that something considerable *is* known about the Supreme Being, whether from reason or revelation, then the Institution in question

> professes every science, and yet leaves out the fore-
> most of them. In a word . . . such an Institution can-
> not be what it professes if there be a God. I do not
> wish to declaim, but by the very force of the terms,
> it is very plain that a Divine Being and a Universi-
> ty so circumstanced [i.e. without theology] cannot
> coexist.[5]

Newman concludes this first point with his usual clarity and precision: "Religious doctrine (theology) is knowledge, in as full a sense as Newton's doctrine is knowledge. University teaching without theology is simply unphilosophical."[6] "Whereas it is the very profession of a University to teach all the sciences, on this account, it cannot exclude theology without being untrue to its profession."[7]

Newman's second point is this: all the sciences are interrelated and have a bearing one on the other; hence, it is impossible to teach them all thoroughly unless all are taken into account, and theology among them. "Moreover," he says, "I have insist-ed on the influence which theology in matter of fact does and must exercise over a great variety of sciences, completing and correcting them; so that, granting it to be a real science occupied upon truth, it cannot be omitted without great prejudice to the teaching of the rest."[8]

His complete argumentation for this point is positively vehe-ment in the face of a world which even a hundred years ago was becoming more and more secularized, where God and the science of God were on the way out, under the influence of such popular thinkers as Bentham, J. Stuart Mill, Darwin, Spencer, and Auguste Comte. Newman recognized the fallacy of their half knowledge that cramped the vision of men. He presented the teaching of theology to laymen as the antidote for this half knowledge, since theology ensures depth of vision, completeness of knowledge, and a divine hierarchy of values.

He recapitulates it thus: "if theology be a branch of knowl-edge, of wide reception, of philosophical structure, of unutterable importance and of supreme influence . . . to withdraw theology from the public schools is to impair the completeness and to invalidate the Trustworthiness of all that is taught in them."[9] "In a word," he concludes, "Religious Truth is not only a portion, but a condition of general knowledge. To blot it out is nothing short of . . . unravelling the web of universal teaching."[10]

Newman's third and last point on the necessity of teaching theology to the layman is nothing short of prophetic. He says that, "supposing theology be not taught, its province will not simply be neglected, but will actually be usurped by other sciences which will teach, without warrant, conclusions of their own in a subject matter [i.e. of theology] which needs its own proper principles for its due formation and dispositions."[11] He clearly demonstrates how the various sciences, without theology, take it upon themselves to pronounce upon matters pertaining to sacred doctrine and morality, passing judgments contrary to divine revelation in matters that exceed the competency of their authority. We have had ample evidence of this development in our day, when a man's competence in any secular field is considered sufficient to give authority to his statements on things religious and moral.

To sum up Newman's case for teaching theology to the layman: (1) The teaching of theology cannot be excluded from the presentation of universal knowledge, for theology is the highest of all sciences, treating of God without whom nothing else in this world is fully intelligible; (2) Theology is essential to the proper orientation of all the other sciences, since all the branches of knowledge form an organic whole, and to remove one science, especially one so fundamental as theology is to impair the unity of the whole structure of knowledge, leaving it truncated and misshapen; (3) The failure to teach theology to the layman leaves a gap in his culture and education that must somehow be filled. It is filled when the function of divine knowledge is usurped by human science, often enough to the detriment of both human science and theology.

The conclusion for us is quite inevitable. If we want complete Christians in the world today, we must present them with a completely Christian view of life. Otherwise there will be, as in fact there are today, Catholics who are great philosophers, great scientists, great artists, great business men, great politicians, but not at the same time great Catholic philosophers, scientists, artists, businessmen, and politicians. G. Howland Shaw, the Laetare Medalist for this year, lamented this fact to me several months ago, and attributed it to the neglect of theology for the layman. In most of our colleges and universities, even Catholic, many laymen have been taught philosophy, science, art, business, and politics without the complete vision of theology. As a result, their knowledge is truly profound in the field of human knowledge, but in the field of divine knowledge they have never progressed beyond the Baltimore Catechism.

This picture is largely negative, but it is a fitting introduction to the second point of this paper.

2. What Kind of Theology Does the Layman Need Most Today?

When we speak of theology, especially of teaching theology, most of us are inclined to think of Tanquerey and Noldin. Possibly too, most of us find it difficult to fit the layman into the picture of our four years in Washington. If we pursue this trend of thought, it may lead us to conclude that Gilson, Maritain, Newman, Shaw, and the rest of them dream beautiful dreams, but are due for a rude awakening if they try to realize them. I would agree with this if we must think of teaching theology to the layman in precisely the same terms as teaching theology to the seminarian.

It is true that theology is theology, but there can be a different approach to its truths, a diversified emphasis on its various branches, a varied order of presentation to meet a new situation. Nor is this a twisting of the science of divine truth to fit our plans. It is merely viewing theology as what it is in the Church—a functional science, dedicated to the service of the Church. It does not detract from the queen of the sciences that it should be considered and taught and learned not only for its own sake, but also for the service of Christ, *cui servire regnare est.*

It is in the Church and in the service of the Church that theology has flourished. It has always been essential to the intellectual training of the cleric because he is dedicated to an active part in the mission of the teaching Church. Now if the cleric's course in theology is adapted to prepare him for his function in the life and work of the Church, it seems logical to propose that the layman too should have his own particular and special course in theology, since he too is called upon, more and more today, to assume an active role in the life and work of the Church, a role specifically different than that of the cleric. Because his place and function in the Church differs from that of the cleric, the layman should not be given a seminarian's course in theology. The layman's course, like the cleric's, should prepare him for his particular and providential role in the life and work of the Church.

This reasoning, of course, brings us to the very practical question: What is the layman's part in the life and work of the Church? The answer to this question is not open to speculation, since the recent Popes have authoritatively declared their minds on the subject. They wish the layman to participate actively in the two great actions of Christ's Mystical Body—in the inner action of public prayer through active participation in the official liturgy of the Church, and in the outer action of apostolate through active participation in the hierarchical apostolate. It is evident that some knowledge of theology is necessary if the layman is to take an intelligent part in these two great manifestations of the Church's life and work, by liturgical and Catholic action. It is also clear that the knowledge of theology required for them is not the same as that demanded of the clergy who have a deeper and broader part in these actions of the Church.

So while there is agreement among most men that the task incumbent on the laity in our secular world today does require some grasp of theology, there is considerable discussion upon the matter of where to place the emphasis, and precisely what kind of a theological course to teach. In a negative way, we can at least say that those elements of theology that are specifically aimed at preparing priests (for example, the casuistic emphasis in moral theology geared to confessional practice) should be eliminated from the layman's course in theology.

To go beyond this negative consideration, and to outline definitively a layman's course in theology is a more difficult proposition. We do know fundamentally what we want. As the eminent modern theologian, John C. Murray puts it, the course in lay theology "must have a characteristic and conscious orientation toward the development in the student of a completely Christian personality, imbued with the total ideal of a Christian lay life, and dedicated to the full vocation of the contemporary Christian man."[12] Murray thinks that one could not give such a course unless well versed in dogma, scripture, liturgy, history, ascetical and mystical theology and the social doctrine of the Church, particularly the papal doctrine on Catholic Action against the background of modern culture.

If we might venture a suggestion, I would say that however the course be formulated, the casting of the curriculum should be completely Christocentric: based on the Mystical Body considered in the complete economy of redemption. My reason for this is that by presenting this one central truth, all the other truths that in any way concern the part of the layman in the life and work of the Church are unified and brought into focus in Christ. This, after all, is the method of Holy Scripture, which is unified in the presentation of Christ's life and work. The life and work of Christ are moreover the sum and substance of both liturgical and Catholic action.

These are but a few indications of the problems involved in a discussion of teaching theology to the layman. We have only attempted to establish the need for such teaching, and to indicate the further work to be done in determining the practical content and extent of this teaching. I do not think that the problems involved should deter us from pursuing a necessary task to completion. Even Protestant thinkers are realizing the tremendous necessity of theology and religion in the world today. D. Elton Trueblood, writing in *Religion and Life*,[13] on the place of theology in a university, suggests that theology should especially be taught to the faculty, and I think his words carry special weight for the lay faculty of a Catholic University. Indiana University in its newsletter for November 1942 stated as the objective of a course in religious instruction there: "To seek in all ways to make religion as intelligent as science, as appealing as art, as vital as the day's work."

While we may not agree entirely with the theological experiment across the road at St. Mary's, that is, as far as content goes, I do not think we can fail to recognize the courageousness of its purpose. In the words of Sr. Madeleva, it is an effort to "make religion the strongest and crowning department in our colleges, to give wisdom its proper place in our curricula, to make our colleges literate in religion and Catholic in essence."

In conclusion, teaching theology to the layman is both a problem and a challenge. While it may, at first, seem to be purely academic and insignificant as compared to the other problems and challenges of our atomic age, I sincerely think that in answering it, we shall be providing the fundamental solution to many of the other problems. And on the basis of this assumption, I do not think that a university will fulfill its noble task to a confused world unless it meets this fundamental problem and answers this challenge by teaching theology to the layman.

If the teaching of theology is a duty of any Institution committed by its very nature to the diffusion and preservation of universal knowledge, it is both a duty and a privilege for a Catholic university whose specific right to existence is bound up in that word *Catholic*, which indicates its complete dedication to the spread of the kingdom of God in the minds and hearts of men.

Notes

1. Étienne Gilson, *Christianisme et Philosophie*, 163.
2. Gilson, p. 165.

3. Jacques Maritain, *Education at the Crossroads* (New Haven, CT: Yale University Press, 1960), 73–75.

4. Maritain, p. 83.

5. John Henry Newman, *The Idea of a University*, 24–25.

6. Newman, 42.

7. Newman, 98.

8. Newman, 98.

9. Newman, 69.

10. Newman, 70.

11. Newman, 70, cf. p. 96.

12. J. C. Murray, S.J., "Towards a Theology for the Layman," *Theological Studies* (1944): 344.

13. D. Elton Trueblood, "The Place of Theology in a University," *Religion and Life* 11, 510–20.

Sermon for the Opening of the School Year
September 23, 1956

And He [Christ] Himself gave some men as apostles, and some as prophets, others again as evangelists, and others as pastors and teachers, in order to perfect the saints for a work of ministry, for building up the body of Christ, until we all attain to the unity of the faith, and of the deep knowledge of the Son of God, to perfect manhood, to the mature measure of the fullness of Christ.
—*Eph 4:11–13*

. . . Some thoughtful people have questioned whether or not the physical growth of America today has been matched by a corresponding development of our spiritual wisdom and moral character. The same question might be asked of Notre Dame, not in a carping spirit of criticism, but in a reflective mood of self-analysis that is linked to the sincere desire for the greatest possible perfection in the high task committed to us. It is certainly no less true of universities, than of men, that the unexamined life is not worth living.

The inner growth of a university depends in large measure upon the excellence of its faculty. This is more than the sum total of their individual talents, however, because a university is a community of scholars working together, not a mere collection of individual good minds, haphazardly and geographically assembled in one place. Now collaborative human effort in a university requires some unity of spirit and ideal, some human understanding and sharing of the great dignity of the endeavor. In the nature of the world we live in, with its often superficial judgments and attitudes, some members of the university community will often receive a larger measure of praise and plaudits for accomplishments that are, in reality, the work of all. Yet, at the heart of the endeavor and in the eyes of God, each member must know that he belongs and is important and vital to the task.

Our opening text from St. Paul addresses itself to this problem, in the exact context of the Church. This is helpful to us too, because Notre Dame is, among other things, a work of the Church and, moreover, the work of Notre Dame highlights one of the great opportunities and deep problems of the Church today: that of priests and laymen working fruitfully together in a common endeavor. There is a meaningful historical and theological background to the position of the laity in the Catholic Church. In modern times, some have accused Catholic laymen of being passive and silent by-standers in the work of the Church. There is some considerable truth in this accusation, and I am not implying that it is entirely the fault of the laymen, or that this is as it should be.

As usual, history gives us an understandable background of the situation. In earliest times, St. Paul spoke with great affection of those laymen who helped him with his great mission to the Gentiles. The situation of a too passive laity in recent centuries is perhaps best explained by the doctrinal emphasis on hierarchical authority following the negation of this authority in the

Reformation, when the preacher was substituted for the priest, when the sermon replaced the Holy Sacrifice, and private interpretation was judged superior to traditional pronouncement. Reemphasis in time of crisis may then have strengthened the position of embattled clergy, but quite another phenomenon is taking place today, and this time it is the laity whose position in the Church is being reaffirmed, again historically in the face of crisis. The crisis of our times is the almost universal divorce of the spiritual from the temporal order. The capital sin of our age is the process of secularism, which someone has aptly described as the practice of the absence of God. In this present crisis, the layman is the key man. The solution to secularism must be a work of mediation between the two orders. The layman is in a perfect position to mediate: as a member of the Church, he is in the spiritual order; and as a layman, he is, by definition, in the temporal order. However, one does not mediate merely by being in a circumstantial position to do so. The layman must understand his position, the true inner nature of the problem, and have the power to act. This is where we leave history and enter theology.

To understand fully the position of the layman in the Church, one must understand the Church. And to understand the Church, one must understand Christ. It would be utter presumption to cover this vast field of theology in so few words, but the main lines of thought may be indicated with the hope that all of you may study the matter more deeply as it deserves, and indeed requires, for full comprehension.

In the fullness of time, God sent his only begotten Son into the world to restore to men full access to eternal union with him, to which all mankind is destined, by the great goodness of God, our Creator. The work of reuniting God and man was also a task of mediation, and Christ, Our Lord, is the great, and in a true sense, the only eternal Mediator of all time. Others can only participate in his work. His basic work of mediation was accomplished for all time in his person, by his Incarnation, wherein the eternal Son of God is born of the Blessed Virgin Mary; God becomes man and dwells among us. God and man are substantially united in his person. The act of sacrificial redemption on Calvary is not the end of the story, but only the beginning of the great drama of redemption and salvation that goes on as long as there are men to be saved. The important part of the story for us this morning is that while Christ's work of redemption and salvation happened once for all, in his divine plan it is applied, man by man, in every age, and every man has his own proper part to play in the redemptive process. It might have been different, but the fact is that Christ wished to associate us with him, and, for this reason, he established his Church, his Mystical Body of which he is the head and we the members. Christ, Our Lord, said that he came to give life and give it more abundantly. The Church is not just a juridical organization, but a life-giving body. We are incorporated into this body by Baptism, reborn to the very divine life of Christ, our head. Through the sacraments, this life is nurtured and grows. We are not independent of each other because we live the same divine life of Christ, our head. In serving others, we serve Christ, and if we should despise another, we despise Christ.

The particular point I would highlight here is that no one is unimportant in the Church, because all of us have the same basic dignity as members of Christ, partakers of his divine life. All truth, all grace, all power, all dignity in the Church, from pope to peasant, is from Christ. And because we share his life, we also share his work of redemption, not all in the same measure, but all truly participate if the redemptive work is to be accomplished as he wishes. This is why the Catholic laity have been exhorted by every recent Holy Father to take active part in the prayer life of the Church through the liturgical movement, that inwardly all of us may grow to the full maturity of the life of Christ together. And because life is manifested by works, there has been a constant appeal for lay participation in the works of the Church through the lay apostolate. In speaking to some pilgrims at Rome, Pius XII recently said, "You do not merely belong to the Church; you are the Church." For the Church ultimately is the presence of Christ in the world today, in each of us, still living and working at the age-long task of bringing God to men and men to God, through Christ and in Christ. And so it may truly be concluded that, to the extent that Christ lives in us, to that extent is our work Christlike and of eternal value.

Against this historical and theological background, I would now like to sketch briefly the task of the layman who lives in the temporal as well as spiritual order. The great danger is two-fold: that the orders be kept absolutely separate, the secularistic scheme of things, or that they be hopelessly confused, as those who would substitute piety in one order for competence in the other. The temporal and spiritual orders are indeed distinct, but certainly need not be separate. Human nature and divine nature are distinct realities in Christ, but united in his person. His humanity did not suffer from the union, but was ineffably glorified and enriched. Nor was divinity diminished, for only by becoming man could Christ give us the supreme evidence of God's love for man by dying for us as a man. Our work, in a modern-secularism world, must be patterned on these great supernatural realities. The layman must have a clear view of both orders if he is to be a Christian humanist in the modern world. The alternative is utter naturalism, or pseudo-supernaturalism. The layman must respect the values of both orders, as well as the proper objectives and techniques of both orders, if his life and work are to have balance and full significance, and if he himself is to be equal to the challenge of secularism.

In the spiritual order, the plane of the Church, the layman's action is directed toward eternal values, toward God and the things of God, toward the goal of eternal life for himself and those about him. Here the layman is engaged in liturgical and apostolic life as a member of the Body of Christ; he offers prayers and sacrifices and indeed participates in the reoffering of the Sacrifice of Christ in the Mass. He practices virtue so that Christ may be manifest in him; he lives his faith and serves with the freedom of the sons of God. This you may say is his life in Christ and God.

In the temporal order, the plane of the world, if you will, the layman's action is directed toward the goods of time. Here the layman acts as a citizen of the earthly city, and he takes his legitimate part in the affairs of humanity in time. The values he works for may be of the intellectual or moral order, they will certainly involve civilization and culture, the works of science or art, the political, economic, and social exigencies of daily living. I would underscore here again that all these are real values. The important work of mediation is this: these earthly values, insofar as they are true and good, may be revivified, elevated, offered to God by the man of the spirit who engages in them. In this way, our activities in the affairs of time will never become final ends. And, on the other hand, we will not be tempted to offer to God a mediocre service in the temporal order, for God is not honored by poor art, shoddy science, shady politics, or a sensualist culture.

What is needed so desperately today is what Maritain calls the integral humanist, the whole man who is really at home, temporarily in time and eternally in eternity, the man who respects both orders, and neglects neither, the man who has been completely revivified by the grace of Christ, whose faith and hope and charity are able to renew, direct, and revivify the things of time, and to achieve the human good in all its fullness in time while ultimately referring it to the eternal good that awaits beyond. This is the man who cherishes the highest wisdom and is not afraid to let it shine through his life and work on the things of time. Without this man, I know not how the elevating and eternal spirit of the Gospel, the saving presence of Christ, is going to be manifest in the many quarters of this modern world where the temporal order and the things of time have become ends in themselves, divorced from any higher wisdom, any nobler law, any breath of God and the things of God.

The world is poorer today for secularism, and will be poorer still if the work of incarnation does not take root in the lives of our laymen. I know of no place where this new breath of divine life could more effectively grow and multiply than here at Notre Dame. Many of our concerns are of the temporal order, but all about us there are reminders that this is not a lasting city. Our work of education is in the world, but never completely of the world. We have priests and laymen side by side; we are committed to a higher wisdom while working effectively for all the perfection that is possible in the things of time. And there is an undefinable spirit of devotion and consecration here that alone can explain what has already been accomplished and the great things that we yet aspire to accomplish.

We began by reading the words of St. Paul to the Ephesians, where he describes how Christ has provided for many functions in his Mystical Body, the Church, and how all of these various functions are for the building up of the Body, until we all attain to the unity of the faith, and of the deep knowledge of the Son of God, to perfect manhood, to the mature measure of the fullness of Christ. I would like to conclude with the words of St. Paul which immediately follow this passage:

> We are no longer to be children, no longer to be like storm-tossed sailors, driven before the wind of each new doctrine that human subtlety, human skill in fabricating lies, may propound. We are to follow the truth, in a spirit of love, and so grow up, in everything, into a due proportion with Christ, who is our head. On Him all the body depends; it is organized and unified by each contact with the source which supplies it; and thus, each limb receiving the active power it needs, it achieves its natural growth, building itself up through love. (Eph 4:14–16)

PART III

LIVES OF FAITH

Faith is a highly personal matter. It has very real consequences. It involves deep commitments, very far beyond geophysics, oceanography, and even solar radiation. Faith gets at us in the depths of our personality and being, what we do or do not believe and why, and what this belief or unbelief does to our lives at the innermost level of our personality.

—Fr. Ted Hesburgh, CSC

In examining how Fr. Ted both experienced and expressed his faith, one can see how faith is often a beautiful thing, but also a thing of paradox: individual and yet communal, dynamic and yet unifying, simple and yet complex, complete surrender and yet ultimate freedom. But above all, true faith is singularly transformational. As Fr. Ted offered, "For this Faith, I am ready to live differently each day . . ." Furthermore, faith is motivational and inspirational. Believers, as Christ-bearers, not only receive for themselves light and life from faith, but the Word and Spirit of God work through them to reflect the truth and radiance of the faith to the world, spreading the hope of salvation and eternal life. While the world often opposes this light, either strongly or subtly, the faithful carry with them Christ's promise of His unwavering Spirit.

This section offers two pieces which illuminate what Fr. Ted saw as grounding tenants of the Catholic faith: "Three Doctrines of Immaculate Conception," with Mary as the Christ-bearer exemplar, and "The Catholic Spirit of Christmas," which centers Christ as the source hope for the faithful. From these fundamental understandings, Fr. Ted's sermon at the inauguration of the Year of Faith delves deeper into the nature and critical importance of individual and collective faith, and his baccalaureate mass sermon from 1971 highlights the challenges to the faith that all believers encounter in the world. Facing temptations and trials constantly, each believer must choose day by day—even moment by moment—if and how to live that faith. After all, as Fr. Ted observed, "There are no conscientious objectors in this encounter . . ."

Three Doctrines of Immaculate Conception
1954

Our theme is at once simple and profound. We have taken as our basic theme the words from the Mass of The Virgin Mary: "Rejoice, O Virgin Mary, thou alone has destroyed all heresies." To illustrate this trust, we have selected three of the key beliefs of Catholics regarding Mary: that she is the Mother of God; that she was conceived without original sin; and that at the end of her life she was assumed bodily into heaven.

All of these beliefs have been defined by the Church as the official belief of Catholics, and each represents a historical landmark in the positive answer of faith to heresy.

The first doctrine of the divine Maternity was defined at the Council of Ephesus in the year 431. It was the definitive answer to four centuries of doubt and controversy about the key doctrine of Christianity: that Christ is true God and true man, that he is one person, eternally proceeding from God the Father, and in time conceived in his humanity by the Virgin Mary. If Mary is the Mother of God, then he is true man, and true God, and one Person. This doctrine is the basis for all the honor given Mary by Catholics, for all we say of her is pale praise beside what God himself has done for her: chosen her to be the Mother of Christ. "He who is mighty has done great things for me and holy is His name" (Lk 1:49).

The second doctrine of the Immaculate Conception defined by Pius IX in 1854 answered all the errors about the soul of man and his redemption that followed during the centuries after the Reformation. When we say that Mary was conceived without original sin, we are saying that all other men are born deprived of divine life and needing redemption. We are clearly defining the natural and supernatural orders and their interrelationships. We are recognizing the state of the soul without redemption, the original sinfulness of Adam, the consequent redemption in

Christ, the God-man. Here is the answer to the easy perfectibility of man, sponsored by Rousseau, to the self-reliance of man expounded earlier by the Pelagians, to the utter corruption of man and consequent pessimistic view of man found in Luther and the neo-orthodox theologians of our day.

The third doctrine of Mary, assumption, defined in 1950 by Pius XII, answers a long accumulation of eros regarding man's body and its relative place in the focus of eternity. Maternalism seems a poor substitute for the fullness of truth when we see Mary receiving, prematurely, the wonderful victory over concupiscence and sensuality that is promised to all of us in the last day at the Resurrection of the body.

The body too is not merely animal, but to be united to the victory of the soul in eternal bliss where human emotions are spiritualized forever.

In all of these doctrines we see Mary as the prototype of what we Christians are meant to be: Christ-bearers, freed from the influence of sin and evil, eternal sharers in the fullness of our humanity, body and soul, with the victory of Christ and Mary at the end of time. She brings us the reality of this promise in herself and in what we believe her to be as a human being: Mother of God, conceived immaculate, assumed bodily into heaven. Surely she alone, in the Providence of God, hers by being what she is, destroyed all heresy.

Sermon (Sacred Heart Church) to Inaugurate a Series of Sermons on the Year of Faith
November 5, 1967

I am very happy to have the opportunity of speaking to the university community this afternoon on the Year of Faith, recently proclaimed by our Holy Father, Pope Paul VI. There will undoubtedly be many who will question why the Holy Father recently declared a "Year of Faith." Unfortunately, people are inclined to question almost everything that comes from Rome these days. One would think that we would be used to such years by now. No one balked at the "International Geophysical Year" or the "Year of the Quiet Sun" or the "Indian Ocean Year." All would welcome other nonscientific years, such as the "Year for Human Rights" or the "Year for World Human Development" or the proposed "International Education Year."

I suppose that the uneasiness in this case comes from the fact that the "Year of Faith" cuts closer to the bone. Faith is a highly personal matter. It has very real consequences. It involves deep commitments, very far beyond geophysics, oceanography, and even solar radiation. Faith gets at *us* in the depths of our personality and being, what we do or do not believe and why, and what this belief or unbelief does to our lives at the innermost level of our personality.

Personally, I am very glad that the Holy Father proclaimed this year, because I think we need it now in a very special way. In the post-Conciliar world, many things are changing and, in a time of rapid change, there need to be a few things which do not change. Faith is one of these. How we express it may be different and with what cultural trappings it is clothed may change from age to age. But what we believe most deeply and most fundamentally as Christians is not a matter of change. Today, many things about the faith tend to get blurred. Faith itself is seen in many new patterns, some very authentic and some highly distorted. In such a setting, faith as construed by some becomes *in* or *out* by personal judgment and interpretation. Faith becomes highly flexible or horribly rigid. All is suddenly black or white. Orthodoxy and heresy are painted in stark contrast, with the result being, for the great broad spectrum of the People of God, confusion.

I will presume to suppose that in the face of these very real contemporary developments our Holy Father wanted us to use a Year of Faith to consider the faith anew, to see what it really is and what it means to you and to me. I can only speak for myself, and I claim no special charisma. But I am here and you are there, and I must testify.

I am not afraid to say to you, openly and simply, that the faith is my most precious possession. It is the one reality which I am prepared, unequivocally at this moment, to follow, even unto death. Till they point the gun or begin the torture or accumulate the temptations that follow all of us in daily life, this must be a qualified testimony, since no man knows the limits of his endurance until he is tried. But, as of this moment, I am prepared to say, "For this faith, I am ready to live differently each day, and to die for it if I must." Any faith less than this is not the faith that the Holy Father speaks of when he proclaims this year. One of the great benefits of this year is that each of you must make your own assessment of your own commitment regarding the Faith.

What has the faith that can demand this fidelity even unto death? Only one ultimate base: the Word of God. (For a more complete treatment of faith and the Word of God read the Vatican Council II documents on Revelation and the Church.) If faith tends to falter, in the life of an individual from time to time, one should first ask: "What does he know of the Word of God?" Not what he knows of the theologians he reads, not what he finds in the religion section of *Time* or *Newsweek*, but what he knows of the pure and unadulterated Word of God. This is what is most important. What is this Word of God? Last week in preparing for this sermon, I reread at one sitting the Gospel of St. John. I had, of course, read it many hundred times in years past, but every time I read it anew it seems to bring something new to me. You might ask, "Why St. John?" I can only say that St. John seems to say something special, in a style different from all of the other Evangelists, Matthew, Mark, and Luke. There is another reason. Some years ago, when speaking to someone who had been in a Siberian labor camp of the Soviet Union, I learned that many of the inmates who were faced with much greater challenges to their faith than any of us have faced to date, were sustained by a tattered, handwritten version of the Gospel of St. John, which passed from hand to hand and was read by flickering candles. This sustained them more than anything else.

In reading St. John, I noticed anew that two words seem to form a kind of leitmotif of everything that he writes appealing to our faith. These two words are *life* and *light*. As I read, I marked some passages that I would like to read to you now. As I read them, I trust you will listen to them as addressed directly to you and remember that they are not really my words, but the Word of God.

St. John's Gospel begins by envisioning what the Word of God means as it was declared in his day. His Gospel opens with the words, "At the beginning of time the Word already was; and God had the Word abiding with Him, and the Word was God. He abode, at the beginning of time, with God. It was through Him that all things came into being, and without Him came nothing that has come to be. In Him there was life, and that life was the light of men. And the light shines in darkness, a darkness which was not able to comprehend it" (vv. 1–5).

A few lines later on, St. John says that all of those who did welcome Our Lord and receive his Words became the Children of God. This is our true vocation.

In chapter 3, St. John writes "God so loved the world, that He gave his only begotten Son, so that those who believe in Him may not perish, but have eternal life. When God sent His Son into the world, it was not to reject the world, but so that the world might find salvation through Him. For the man who believes in Him, there is no rejection; the man who does not believe is already rejected; he has not found faith in the name of God's only-begotten Son. Rejection lies in this, that when the light came into the world men preferred darkness to light; preferred it, because their doings were evil. Anyone who acts shamefully hates the light, will not come into the light, for fear that his doings will be found out. Whereas the man whose life is true comes to the light, so that his deeds may be seen for what they are, deeds done in God" (vv. 16–21).

At the end of chapter 3, St. John says "The man who does accept His witness has declared, once for all, that God cannot lie, since the words spoken by Him whom God has sent are God's own words; so boundless is the gift God makes of His Spirit. The Father loves His Son, and so has given everything into His hands; and he who believes in the Son possesses eternal life, whereas he who refuses to believe in the Son will never see life; God's displeasure hangs over him continually" (vv. 33–36).

In chapter 4, I marked two passages:

> Believe Me when I tell you this; the man who has faith in Me enjoys eternal life. It is I who am the bread of life. Your fathers, who ate manna in the desert, died none the less; the bread which comes down from heaven is such that he who eats of it never dies. I myself am the living bread that has come down from heaven. If anyone eats of this bread, he shall live forever. And now, what is this bread which I am to give? It is My flesh, given for the life of the world. . . . The man who eats this bread will live eternally. (vv. 47–52, 59)

And later on in chapter 6, St. John says, "After this, many of His disciples went back to their old ways, and walked no more in His company. Whereupon Jesus said to the twelve, Would you, too, go away? Simon Peter answered Him, Lord, to whom should we go? Thy words are the words of eternal life; we have learned to believe, and are assured that Thou art the Christ, the Son of God" (vv. 67–71).

In chapter 8, we find these words: "And now once more Jesus spoke to them, I am the light of the world, He said. He who follows Me can never walk in darkness; he will possess the light which is life" (v. 12).

Later on in this chapter, he says: "Believe Me when I tell you this; if a man is true to My word, to all eternity he will never see death" (v. 51).

In chapter 9, there is the wonderful sentence which reads: "As long as I am in the world, I am the world's light" (v. 5).

In chapter 11, St. John says: "Jesus said to her, I am the resurrection and life; he who believes in Me, though he is dead, will live on, and whoever has life, and has faith in Me, to all eternity cannot die" (vv. 25–27).

My last two citations are from chapter 12 of St. John. In verse 24, he says, "Believe Me when I tell you this; a grain of wheat must fall into the ground and die, or else it remains nothing more than a grain of wheat; but if it dies, then it yields rich fruit. He who loves his life will lose it; he who is an enemy to his own life in this world will keep it, so as to live eternally. If anyone is to be My servant, he must follow My way; so shall My servant too be where I am" (vv. 24–26).

A few lines later he says:

> If only I am lifted up from the earth, I will attract all men to Myself. . . . I have come into the world as a light, so that all those who believe in Me may continue no longer in darkness. If a man hears My words, and does not keep true to them, I do not pass sentence on him; I have come to save the world, not to pass sentence on the world. The man who makes Me of no account, and does not accept My words, has a judge appointed to try him; it is the message I have uttered that will be his judge at the last day. And this, because it is not of My own impulse that I have spoken; it was My Father who sent Me what words I was to say, what message I was to utter. And I know well that what He commands is eternal life; everything then, which I utter, I utter as My Father has bidden Me. (vv. 33, 46–50)

I have cited these words of St. John because so often one speaks of faith without speaking of the root of faith which is God's Word. You may have thought at times whether Our Lord really knew what would happen to his Word once it was proclaimed to the world. He did indeed know and spelled it out for us in a wonderful parable, which is found in chapter 8 of St. Luke's Gospel:

> A sower went out to sow his seed. And as he sowed, there were some grains that fell beside the path, so that they were trodden underfoot, and the birds flew down and ate them. And others fell on the rocks, where they withered as soon as they were up, because they had no moisture. And some fell among briers, and the briers grew up with them and smothered them. But others fell where the soil was good, and when these grew up they yielded a hundredfold. So saying this, He cried aloud, "Listen, you that have ears to hear with." (vv. 5–8)

We are told that his disciples asked him what this parable meant. Our Lord told them that:

> *The seed is God's word.* Those by the wayside hear the word, and then the devil comes and takes it away from their hearts, so that they cannot find faith and be saved. Those on the rock are those who entertain the word with joy as soon as they hear it, and yet have no roots; they last for a while, but in time of temptation they fall away. And the grain that fell among the briers stands for those who hear it, and then, going on their way, are stifled by the cares, the riches, and the pleasures of life, and never reach maturity. And the grain that fell in good soil stands for those who hear the word, and hold by it with a noble and generous heart, and endure, and yield a harvest. (vv. 12–15)

Even knowing that all would not accept his Word, or believe and have faith, Our Lord still perdured unto the end and gave to his apostles the task of preaching the Word, the good news of salvation, to the whole of creation. We find this in the final words of the Gospel of St. Mark: "Then at last He appeared to all eleven of them as they sat at table, and reproached them with their unbelief and their obstinacy of heart, in giving no credit to those who had seen Him after He had risen. And He said to them, 'Go out all over the world, and preach the gospel to the whole of creation; he who believes and is baptized will be saved; he who refuses belief will be condemned'" (vv. 14–16).

So it is that this Year of Faith brings us back to look at the taproots of our Christian belief, to the sources of light and life of which St. John spoke, to baptism and our faith, to the two essential elements of our Salvation in time and in eternity.

Faith goes much deeper than the surface realities that so often concern us: Whether we pray in Latin or in English, whether we use black or purple vestments, organs or guitars, whether we sing Gregorian Chant or folk music, whether our Eucharistic bread is made of whole wheat or bleached white flour. These are not really matters of faith or of our fundamental commitment in faith. Faith begins at the simple Word of God, as spoken to us by his Incarnate Son, and expanded in us by his Holy Spirit. Faith is our ultimate and deepest assurance that God is our Father and that we can speak to him as such, and that Jesus Christ is our Brother and that all others are our brothers in Christ, and that the Holy Spirit is our Light and our daily inspiration, if we will accept him.

Faith takes us as we are and illumines our mind beyond where it can reach by itself. Faith expands our questing to God himself and enlarges our intellectual horizons beyond time to eternity. Faith teaches us that by baptism we were born again of the Holy Spirit, a phrase used by God's Word as well in describing the birth of his Son from his Virgin Mother, Mary. Faith assures us, again by God's Word, that this rebirth is unto everlasting life and that as members of Christ's Church this eternal life is ours right now in the depths of our souls, and that we grow in it by following Christ Our Lord, as our Truth, our Way, and our very Life. All prayer and all the Sacraments are means to this end, to join us to Christ, to undergird our hope, which is impossible without faith, and to deepen our love for God and man, which also depends on our Faith. Faith also buttresses human freedom, which is a fragile thing, so open to evil as well as to good, so easily depressed by frustration, so alone without the strength of God's grace and the promise of his Word.

Faith is then a key to another world, a key we did not earn, but was given to us freely by Our Savior, a key which we can indeed lose if we do not cherish it, live it, and strengthen it by all the means that the good Lord gave us, particularly by meditating on his Word. The greatest of all human tragedies today is not the holocaust of Vietnam, not the threat of thermo-nuclear war, not the inhumanities that accompany civil rights movements, not social injustice and charity, but that some people gave up their faith so easily, for such silly reasons, while others are willing to die for it. What is really tragic today is that in losing the faith, if we are to believe God's Word, it is really eternal life and all hope that is lost.

Faith is the one great quality that Christ Our Lord required of all those whom he encountered as he walked the hot and dusty paths of Judea and Galilee. How often he said, after giving sight to the blind, health to the sick, forgiveness to the sinner: Thy faith has made thee whole.

And the same words are true of each of us today: whatever our anguishes, our difficulties, or our frustrations because of what our Faith requires of us, we can say humbly to Christ, "Lord, I do believe, help my unbelief," and, believing him, despite all of our faults and imperfections, we will indeed be made whole again. With faith, our minds will be enlightened by his great light, our petty, busy, fragile lives filled with his eternal life, even now, and certainly unto eternity where eternal life and light will at last dispel all the darkness and all the binding human limitations of temporal life and death. Then we will no longer need faith or a Year of Faith for we shall see. We may indeed see now, in a glass darkly, as through the dark stained-glass windows of this church as evening comes upon us, but then, "In His light we shall see the Light." And more than this, we shall live, for all I have said to you today is summed up better in another sentence which is also part of the Word of God, in which Our Lord expressed to us the whole meaning of his life on earth and now in his Church: "I have come that you may have life, and have it more abundantly."

Sermon at Baccalaureate Mass, University of Notre Dame
May 22, 1971

The Epistle today reminds us that, while this day is a special point in history for each of you, a completion of what is past and a commencement of what is yet to come, God for each of us extends across the whole spectrum of our lives as the Alpha and Omega (A to Z for those who never studied Greek), the First and the Last, the Beginning and the End. Somehow, God presided mysteriously over those first moments of our human existence, and he will be with us at the end, as during all the days in between—whether we notice his presence or not. St. John also assures us that the award, at the end, as today, will be what we have deserved.

If the Epistle had included the next verse that follows this, you would have had a warning—that while some will in reward enter the Eternal City, others must stay outside, and they are listed: "dogs, fortune-tellers, and fornicators, and murderers, and idolaters, and every one of false speech and false life."

It is a curious list—the dogs must be sons of you-know-whats; the fortune-tellers I leave to your imagination, although I suspect they are those who predict a great future for you—with little effort on your part; the fornicators are those who have not learned how to distinguish between selfish sensuality and true love; the murderers, those who follow Cain and his works of violence; the idolaters, those who confuse God with a whole variety of created goods that they variously worship—money, power, pleasure, whatever—and, last, everyone of false speech and false life.

This latter category is made up of all those whose life is ruled by something other than integrity and conscience. Here, I am moved to quote to you the words of Sir Winston Churchill that I have addressed to long generations of Notre Dame graduates: "The only guide to a man is his conscience; the only shield to his memory is the rectitude and sincerity of his actions. It is very imprudent to walk through life without this shield, because we are so often mocked by the failure of our hopes and the upsetting of our calculations; but with this shield, however the fates may play, we march always in the ranks of honor."

Today is, among other things, a day of judgment, not last, but intermediate judgment. May you all be as successful in the final judgment on your lives which will be so much more revealing and more important than today's judgment which is transitory and temporal, while the final judgment will be ultimate and eternal.

Now to the Gospel, which is full of joy and hope for those who have ears to hear. Our Savior is having a final word with his followers at the Last Supper, which we commemorate here in the Mass. We are part of that small group around the table, if we truly follow Christ, Our Savior, as they did down those long dusty roads of Judea and Galilee. He assures us that he has lost none except Judas, who chose to be lost. He wants to share eternal joy with us who follow him, even though the world may hate us for following him. He does not want us, for all that, to remove ourselves from the world, but to live in the world with faith and honor and in truth which is his Word. In fact, he tells us, most appropriately for today, that we are being *sent* into the world, consecrated in truth. He prays not only for us, who will find this life in truth—the opposite of those the Epistle condemned for false words and false life—but Our Savior prays as well for those in the world who through us will find the truth, as they see our lives which reflect his truth, the truth of those who have faith in Christ, Our Lord.

He commits to us who follow him and his message the task of creating unity in a divided world—the unity of love, love of God for us, love of each of us for the other. He also speaks of the Christian life lived in faith and love, and hope, too. Finally, he tells us that he will be with us all the way, which is our pledge of strength and love shared, and of the glory to come.

You may at this moment judge yourself unworthy, or even unprepared for this difficult undertaking. Some may even be uninterested in taking part. But the invitation is always there, the spiritual battle is already joined in your own life and in the world that lies ahead for each of you. There are no conscientious objectors in this encounter, only those who live their lives in Christ and those who reject it to their own eternal peril. You are perfectly free to follow either path, but not free to avoid the consequences of your decision.

The days ahead will have their lessons for each of you, some joyfully learned, like lessons of love, and some that will etch your very souls with the strong acid of sorrow and adversity. We trust that the values you have seen or learned here at Notre Dame will sustain you in adversity: the joy of seeing the truth, the exhilaration of beauty, the innate strength of goodness, the passion for justice in our times, the quiet courage born of prayer, the love and compassion we owe all humans who suffer, the competence and commitment to do something to bring a better world to birth, the modesty and humility that our human frailty dictates, the respect we owe to all things truly human, sensitivity to spiritual realities, sorrow for our sins, and hope for God's mercy, in a word, salvation, ours and the world's.

Our hope and prayer for each of you today is that all of these great intellectual and moral qualities will deepen their roots in your life and grow through all the days given to each of you, wherever you may be, whatever you may do, to enrich each of you as a person born and nourished in faith, to add luminosity to your lives in a world often sunken in darkness.

The final Word of Christ, Our Savior, was to promise his Spirit to each of you. If I might speak in the person of Christ to each of you this day, may I suggest that whatever your present spiritual weakness or strength as you face the future—most of the original disciples were very weak—you remember in the days ahead how to cry for help when you need it. It is a simple prayer—three words—but it calls on the final promise of Our Lord: Come, Holy Spirit. Call, and he will come, and, with him, you will not fail whatever the odds—which is good Notre Dame language.

My own personal assessment is that the odds are going to be fairly formidable in the years ahead for all of us. The fortune-tellers mentioned above will be promising you easy salvation, with a minimum of discipline, sacrifice, and tough moral decisions in your personal life. Salvation never was easy, nor is the true pursuit of happiness and inner peace, both of which are not unrelated to salvation. St. Paul puts it bluntly: as you sow, so shall you reap. Sow in the flesh and you reap corruption. Sow in the spirit and you reap life everlasting. And remember, God is not mocked, least of all by his free and intelligent creatures.

The odds do not only bear on our personal life and salvation—the difficult daily call to personal honor and integrity—but we will live increasingly in institutions, civil, religious, familial, that are rocked by rapid and, at times, cataclysmic change. We cannot for long resign from the human race and all human institutions. Nor should we. It is a far better strategy to work for constructive institutional changes that are responsive to the good winds of renewal that sweep the modern world. We have had enough of apathy and cynicism—turning-off and copping-out, in your idiom. My advice for you is to turn to and cope.

In all of this personal and social endeavor that lies ahead of you, the Holy Spirit, for whom we yearn again during this season, as did the disciples in the Upper Room, is still our best assurance of wisdom, vision, and courage, inspiring the true kind of personal conscience that seeks first the kingdom of God and his justice, not our personal whim and convenience. Come, Holy Spirit.

We watch you go forward with deep pride and true affection May Our Blessed Mother, Notre Dame, bless you always with her wonderful Child.

The Catholic Spirit of Christmas
No Date

To arrive at the Catholic spirit of Christmas, one must first move patiently and prayerfully through Advent, meditating on the great wonder that will come to pass. Today, the reality of the Incarnation has been all but smothered with artificiality. We live in a world that bypasses this holy preparation; that substitutes cosmetic trappings and romantic tinsel for the great truth—at once stark and sublime—of the Christmas story. Charles Dickens's character, Scrooge, called England's thoroughly material celebration of Christmas, "Humbug!" And later, George Bernard Shaw dismissed the joyful season as a "conspiracy of shopkeepers." They were both unedifying, but terribly accurate, in their appraisal of the commercial travesty it had become in many quarters.

For the Catholic, all history revolves around that event which is central in liturgy as it is in life. Christmas is the birthday of an era, the inauguration of a culture, the beginning of a creed, the fountainhead of man's hope. The Catholic spirit of Christmas clings to the central character—a little boy who was God—born in an unlovely hovel where cattle sheltered against the weather; born of a mother who was a virgin. He came at a time when she was traveling. Her first guests were rough, uncouth shepherds, as wild as the wilderness itself, tousle-haired and tangle-bearded. His Mother knew inconvenience and hunger, endured failure, dejection, derision. Yet she was joyfully aware that her Child is God; that his Incarnation is real; that God is with us, not merely as a stranger on a perfunctory state visit, but as a sharer of our nature and our lot.

Hence, the Catholic spirit of Christmas, to its last fiber, is dyed in divinity. Our Christmas begins at the stable, takes note of the characters in the drama, and closes with the quiet realization that God has come to redeem his people. How meaningless is the occasion without the central figure—the Christ Child! He is the imperishable beauty of the face of Christmas.

This tremendous spiritual truth underlies the origin, meaning, and purpose of all our Christmas customs and our rejoicing. It is a *holiday* only because it is first a *holy day*—the day on which Christ, the Son of God, became Man. And this Catholic spirit remains today what it was originally—the happy recollection of the coming of the Savior. And it is only by recalling the birth of Our Lord that we take renewed courage to sing: "Glory to God in the highest; and on earth peace to men of good will!"

PART IV

LIVES OF PRAYER

People have a lot of funny ideas about prayer. You don't have to be on your knees to pray, nor do you need a gilt-edged prayer book. Real prayer is simply talking with God, who has a personal interest in each one of you and is only too glad to listen to you and to help you whenever you speak up and ask for help.

—*Fr. Ted Hesburgh, CSC*

As evident in Fr. Ted's private and public faith, prayer is as simple, as constant, and as utterly vital to life as breathing. One can experience a remarkable and perhaps unexpected intimacy in communicating with the God of the Universe, approaching God in humility, gratitude, and total confidence as a beloved child of God. According to Fr. Ted, prayer can involve any topic under the sun and need not be limited to generalities. Believers can praise specific attributes of God, express gratitude for specific blessings, and ask for specific help, especially such spiritual gifts as wisdom, joy, peace, courage, and patience. Moreover, the faithful can step into intercessory roles reflective of Christ the High Priest and the Blessed Virgin, seeking mercy, favor, and help for fellow believers and for a world desperately in need of hope.

This section begins with an address delivered originally to students at a women's college, Fr. Ted's "Where to Get Help," which dismantles common misconceptions or obstacles to a vibrant prayer life and instead presents prayer as a relational, essential, and life-giving practice. This section moves then to examples of Fr. Ted's own prayer life, showing his extraordinarily personal connection to God that could not help but emerge even in his most public of prayers, whether offering the invocation of the 1955 YPO Convention or blessing the inauguration of university presidents or beginning yet another academic year at the University of Notre Dame. Keenly aware as he was of his own roles and responsibilities as well as those of the people for whom he prayed, Fr. Ted forever presented himself rightly before God as a man—and a people—in need of help. In his words, "We begin again in prayer and confidence—perhaps better said, confident because we pray."

Where to Get Help
1952

How many times in life do you feel the problems piling up, solutions hard to find, and you wonder: now where am I going to get help?

The biggest help, of course, comes from God, whose care follows you wherever you go and whatever you do. And the best way to get a healthy share of his help is by prayer and the sacraments.

People have a lot of funny ideas about prayer. You don't have to be on your knees to pray, nor do you need a gilt-edged prayer book. Real prayer is simply talking with God, who has a personal interest in each one of you and is only too glad to listen to you and to help you whenever you speak up and ask for help.

It is a wonderful idea to start off the day with a prayer—not necessarily a long string, but just a few words, like, "Thanks for bringing me through the night, Lord. I'd like to live this new day with you, doing everything your way, with you and for you. Please stay with me all day long and help me. Don't let me do anything you can't do with me." There's a nifty prayer in four sentences. If you say it on your knees, you'll probably remind a few others to say good morning to God. I heard just the other day about a boy who came into the Church, because the first night he spent in a Catholic school, he saw the other lads kneeling down beside their beds to say their prayers before turning in. He thought only little boys did this, and it made a great impression on him.

You should say hello to God during the day, too. It doesn't matter where you are or what you are doing. You can speak to God while getting on a bus, sitting at the typewriter, or waiting for an elevator. The great truth is that we can contact God at any time with a short glance or thought or word in his direction. This habit of prayer can fill your deity with strength, for in looking to God from time to time as the day goes by, you will especially learn to look to him in times of trial and temptation and trouble.

Once you realize that Christ really lives within you, and you try sincerely to live your life with him, doing everything as he wants to do it with you, then you turn your whole life into a prayer. Like King Midas in the fable, you turn everything you touch into gold—only, your gold is eternal. This continual contact with God through prayer gives real depth and richness to your life, which can otherwise be drab and empty and rather purposeless. Sometimes people wonder what to speak to God about. The simplest answer to that one is to speak to him about himself and yourself. Certainly if you know who God is, it won't seem so surprising that you should adore him and tell him you love him. And if you begin to realize all he has done for you, you won't find it so strange that you should say thanks once in a while. And if you're like every human being who has made some mistakes, it will be the most natural thing in the world to tell him you are sorry and ask him for the strength to do better in the future. And then there are those hundred and one things we need every day. That brings us to the easiest type of prayer, the kind in which we ask God for all the things we need.

One of the great things you can thank God for, as a Catholic, is the fact that you have the sacraments at your disposal. If you got down on your knees and stayed there for the next hundred years or so, you couldn't begin to thank God for the great grace he has afforded you, in giving you Confession, Mass, and Holy Communion so that you could partake of his strength and face life with him.

Always remember that these sacraments are yours to use. They are not given as a reward for virtue, but as a means of helping you to be good.

Some girls seem to make a torture of Confession. God never meant it to be that. He really instituted the Sacrament of Confession to help you stay close to him. All he wants is that you frankly admit your faults, humbly and sincerely as you see them. The priest is there to help with any difficulties and clear up any doubts. And, of course, the most important thing of all is to be really sorry for your past sins, when you confess them, and to be determined to start off anew with Christ Our Lord, and to do better with the help of his grace. With the absolution that comes from Confession, you get the grace and the strength and the power of Christ to do better. Confession isn't just a means for white-washing your sins. It's more like a blood transfusion, giving you new strength and vigor to keep on trying, not to get discouraged, because Christ Our Lord walks out of the box with you. If you sincerely do your best, facing life with him, you can't lose.

Of course, all of this doesn't make it easier to kneel down and admit you made mistakes. God doesn't ask that it be easy for you, but only that you have the candor and sincerity to admit that you have made mistakes, and then to ask for help that you need to do better. Confession can bring you all these things, and will also bring you the deep peace of soul that comes from knowing you stand right with God. That in itself is a great blessing.

Mass and Holy Communion are great sources of strength, too. Some girls start slipping on Sunday Mass when they are away from home. But you have all the more reason to be faithful now that your needs are greater. Remember, God thinks of you and cares for you every moment of every day. The half hour you give back to him on Sundays isn't much compared to that. Even though it will mean missing some sleep when you're tired after a Saturday night dance, be faithful, and God will be faithful to you when you need some extra help some day.

If you appreciate what the Mass is, you'll be at Mass whenever it's humanly possible to be there, even through the week. Don't just sit and watch the Mass either. Offer it up with the priest. Bring your personal offerings if you want to make it worthwhile. Bring to Mass all the trials and errors, all the joys and sorrow of the day, and the week. Like the little drop of water mingled with the wine at the Offertory, the weak water of your little sacrifice is mingled with the strong wine of Christ's sacrifice. Both of them are consecrated and offered to God together. Then your sacrifice becomes really worthwhile, as it is joined with the greatest Sacrifice of all time, the Sacrifice of Calvary which is renewed at the altar by the priest.

It is typical of the generosity of God that when you offer the gift of yourself and your days to God in the Mass, he closes the Mass by giving you the Gift of gifts, himself. Holy Communion means perfect, inexpressible contact with God. He is there within you, all your own. Lay your needs at his feet, thank him for living your days with you. Tell him you're sorry for the things you did without him and against his law. But, above all, tell him you're glad to be so close to him now, and tell him you want him to be your all. Ask him to stay with you as the days go on. And when you're lonesome or homesick, recall that Christ in Holy Communion unites you to your family and your friends who receive the same Lord, though many miles away. After receiving Holy Communion, you get up from your knees strong with the strength of God, courageous with his courage, inwardly beautiful with his beauty. You can't have all this help and fail to make the most of life, for you and Christ make an unbeatable team.

Of course, I've only been talking now about two of the seven Sacraments, and I haven't even said one word about Baptism in which you received the life of God in your soul, or Confirmation that makes you an apostle of Christ, a strong and mature Christian. Well, Rome wasn't built in a day. Suppose I conclude by saying that if you stay close to Our Lord through prayer and the sacraments, I am absolutely sure that all will be well with you. If God is with you, who can be against you? When you are close to him, you'll never have to ask that question that we began with: "Where to get help . . ."

Invocation at YPO Annual Convention
March 31, 1955

As we begin our annual meeting this year, I am indeed honored to voice for all of you a simple invocation for the blessings of Almighty God upon all of us and upon those with whom we work here and at home.

If I might particularize the specific blessings that we young presidents seek, I would ask that we be granted an abundance of those special virtues that characterize good administrators—that by God's grace and the consecrated use of our talents, we may be equal to the opportunity that is ours in these times.

First, Lord, grant us the virtue of *vision*. This is the virtue of ancient prophets and of old wise men. Vision is generally unusual among young men. But, we need vision most of all today, to see and appreciate the whole wide range of opportunities that are especially open to us as young presidents here in America.

Vision shows us clearly that our dealings are not merely with dollars and cents, materials and services. Our basic concern must be with people, human beings, fellow Americans. People, old and young, intelligent and stupid, handsome and ugly, rich and poor, good and bad. Here our work begins and ends, has merit or fault, profit or loss.

In a sense, industry may be said to begin in the damp depths of our mines, on the green and golden plains of our vast land, in the cool shadows of our virgin forests, along our lush river valleys, and across the snowy crests of our mountain ranges. But this good earth and rich land yields only the raw and un-fashioned gifts of nature—the basic minerals, foods, and fibers that are wondrously transformed by man and his industry.

It is man who brings these many gifts to light, who uses his mind and hands, with consummate skill, to perfect and produce, to fashion and to mold. And it is man who buys and sells and uses these fashioned gifts of God for the good life here on earth, a figure of life eternal. Without man, this marvelous land of

America would be undiscovered, undeveloped, and unused. And God himself would be less praised in the absence of our cheery homes, filled with the noise and laughter of happy children.

Lord, we would be failures as presidents, young or old, if we lacked this vision of how industry has helped to make America a bright and wholesome land where people are prized as our greatest resource, the inner strength of our nation. America would be an empty, cheerless place without our millions of happy, secure people, bearing proudly the dignity and likeness of sons of God.

At night, Lord, when we fly above this vast land, we see on all sides, like so many scintillating jewels in the darkness, the many communities that make up America—the twinkling lights of tiny hamlets, the sparkling suburbs, the colorful thoroughfares of our great cities, the bursts of light from our great industrial centers. Show us, Lord, that we have a part in all of this—in the warmth of good families, in the fruitful production of industry, in the order of good government—in all the joy and security and fulfillment of human life for all here in America.

Of old, it was slaves that quarried the rock, turned the mill, and erected against a desert sky the empty hated monuments to the few who selfishly ruled, exploiting God's gifts and God's people, so that a few might rustle in silk while millions shivered in rags. Few, too, it was who lived in marble palaces while millions groveled in foul hovels; few were sated with delicacies while millions eked out an animal-like existence in starvation and famine.

Such has not been and is not the vision of those who preside in America. Our greatest monument is our living society of the free, the challenge of equal opportunity, the aristocracy of talent, and ability and hard work, not of birth, or family, or race.

It is such a vision that you have placed in our hearts, O Lord, for you have fashioned us and all men after your own image and likeness, to be free, not slave, to walk with head held high, not face to earth like brute animals. Grant us, Lord, the vision to see that all we do as presidents can lift men yet higher in actual dignity. Grant us the vision to see that we can, by our deeds, grace this living monument—our free American society of men who walk with dignity while they work with us. Give us the vision to make America an ever brighter beacon in a world still darkened in too many places by un-human slavery and human oppression.

Our balance sheets can never tell the warm story of this human aspect of our work. Let the record be written in the hearts of those who work with us and for us—who share with us the glory of making this great vision of America under God come true.

Buttress our vision, Lord, with the other virtues that must form part of our character as young presidents—if the vision of America is to be realized today and tomorrow under our guidance.

Grant us the virtue of *understanding*—to understand ourselves and our fellow Americans who work with us. In understanding ourselves let us see our faults as well as our virtues. Let us see that we can and do make mistakes which we do need help from the strength and counsel and companionship of others, even though our positions are essentially lonely by nature of our being alone at the top of our organizations.

Keep far from us the stupid pride that would deceive us into seeing ourselves as self-sufficient supermen, infallible geniuses, indispensable giants. Help us remember that the best of us will be quickly replaced and soon forgotten after we die.

In understanding our fellow men and women, let us see first what we can do for them, not just what they can do for us. Help us to understand that true leadership ennobles others in leading, does not exploit others for personal selfish purposes. Help us also to understand the faults and weaknesses of those who work with us, not to ridicule or overly criticize, but to help and to guide and to strengthen. Let us understand that others can be better and happier and thus more productive and fruitful in their lives if they receive the proper encouragement and guidance from us.

All this is made possible by a sincere and warmly human spirit of understanding—that sees the good, the promising, the potential in everyone, not just the bad, the negative, and the weakness. Make each one of us—the understanding president—the man who builds, inspires, and truly leads.

Join this great virtue of understanding with the consequent virtues of humility and patience—humility that we may see ourselves as we are, not better, but no worse either. Let us be neither overbearing nor pessimistic, but just able to live patiently with the reality of ourselves as we are, doing all we can today, but able to put off some things for tomorrow, and still to sleep soundly tonight.

Let these virtues of humility and patience characterize our dealings with others, too, Lord, so that they will not find us always on a throne of our own supposed perfection, or just emerging from the pit of despondency. Grant us the balance to be what we are, patient with what we find in ourselves and in others around us, willing to live patiently with the inevitable mistakes of others because we have learned to live with our own failings.

Help us to do all this and still improve, Lord. And when we have done all that we reasonably can do with ourselves and with those around us, then let us honestly and humbly recognize what we cannot do, and let us be patient enough to live with that reality and still begin another day without envy, or rancor, or discontent. And let us be grateful for what we are, and for the people who work with us—for while we and they might be better, we and they could also be much worse. Let us always remember the unhappy man without shoes who felt sorry for himself, until he saw another man without feet. In our gratitude, let us particularly remember those we love and those that love us.

Lord, there are two other virtues we need if we are to lead as we should and as the times demand: the virtues of integrity and courage. Grant us the personal integrity to recognize always what is right and just, and fill us with the moral courage always to do what is right and just, even though this might be unpopular and difficult and even costly.

Our elders have not always given us good example in this, Lord. Too often the business decision has reflected the expedient, or the obviously profitable, or the easy way out—without reference to whether it was also the just or the right thing to do. We are always under pressure to follow the line of least resistance, Lord. We all like to be popular. We do have to balance the budget and to show a profit, but give us that rare kind of courage that reflects integrity—the courage to look behind popularity and profit to the most important aspect of any transaction—what is right and just in the situation. Once we have decided that question, Lord, give us the courage to follow through, no matter what the pressures in any other direction, for any other reason.

And give us the ancient wisdom to know, Lord, that in business or in any other human endeavor, integrity and courage are the best reputation we can have among men, for honest and courageous men have no price on their souls and no fear in their hearts.

If we always courageously do what is right and what is just, our profit will, in the long run, be beyond dollars and cents, but will include them too. Our popularity will be based on something more solid than our ability to cut corners, and our services will be in demand whenever something really important and difficult is at stake.

As young presidents, Lord, we have even greater need for these virtues of integrity and courage. We need them so that even older people below us can look up to us with pride and confidence and can be happy to follow us, not deterred because of our age, since what we stand for is ageless and priceless in any age.

Lord, we have asked for a lot of virtues here, but really all we are asking for is one thing—the character we need to do our jobs—the vision to see our opportunities, the understanding to see ourselves and others as we are, the humility to live and work with ourselves and others as we are, the patience to be satisfied with what can be done in a human way, the integrity to see what is right and just, and the courage to be men of integrity no matter what the difficulty involved.

Suppose you grant us all these virtues, Lord, what profit will there be in us? Maybe not a lot, Lord, but surely some. Surely, with all of these qualities, and with so many of us in positions at the top of so many enterprises, some good should result for a great number of people and for America. We ask You only to give us a chance, Lord. We are young enough not to be stodgy, stuff-shirted, and ultra-conservative. We are new enough at this president business not to be deeply rutted in bad habits and stubbornly backward attitudes. And finally, Lord, we have enough youthful energy and enough of the idealism and optimism of youth to commit ourselves to the best in business—the broadest range of our opportunity for the good of America.

Grant that beyond the economic good of our people, we may have a hand in achieving also the spiritual good, the community good, the political good, the human good of all our people.

Many people depend upon us, Lord. We would just like to say tonight that we, too, depend upon you—upon your guidance, to see, your grace, to do, and upon your blessing that alone can fully fructify our efforts.

Invocation at the National Academy of Sciences Centennial
October 22, 1963

. . . If our science were to have one heartfelt prayer in our times, might it be this: that science might become in our day the great liberator, a force for peace in the hands of the scientist, not a scourge for mankind, a demonic destructive power. Lord, thou have in the beginning instructed man to establish dominion over the earth. Through science, man has today the possibility and opportunity of dominion, the power of liberating himself at long last from his ancient enemies of hunger and thirst, grinding poverty and hopelessness, illness and premature death, homelessness and ignorance, and unfounded fears and superstitions. Grant us the wisdom, O Lord, so to dominate ourselves that we may be liberators and not destroyers, creating harbingers of hope not specters of the ultimate destruction.

Grant us, O Lord, the understanding to work together, across all the boundaries of nation, culture, and creed, so that we may truly unite the world in hope rather than separate men by an abyss of fear.

Grant us, O Lord, deep reference for all that is and, especially, for what exists beyond the pale of science: the inner dignity of man that science is to serve, not abuse.

And, finally, deliver us, O Lord, from all arrogance because, for all our power, we still need thee and each other; for all we know, there is yet a vast universe of things unknown; for all our deepest yearnings in time, there is still a deeper hunger for the unending fullness of eternity, when darkness will truly become light, when life will be freed of its finite chains, when in possessing thee, we will truly possess together, in knowledge and love, the whole universe that we now see in a glass, darkly.

Bless this day, O Lord we pray. Bless us and bless our hopes and grant us peace in our times.

Invocation at Inauguration of Dr. Paul Cook as President of Wabash College
December 3, 1966

Heavenly Father, Lord of Wisdom and Might, we pray to You for a blessing upon this assembly and upon the purposes it represents. In a day and at a time when leadership is sorely needed, we have witnessed the installation of a new leader who will now carry in his heart, in his mind, and upon his shoulders too, the hope and the destiny and the continuation of the long and honorable tradition of learning at Wabash College. We pray that he may be blessed with all the qualities of wisdom and understanding that liken us, even in our humble and finite way, to You who are the ultimate source of all wisdom and understanding. We pray that he may be ever endowed with the power to inspire all those at the heart of this noble endeavor, the faculty and the students, the administration, the Trustees, and the benefactors, too. Especially, we ask for President Paul Cook the grace to see and the fortitude to follow the course of wisdom and justice and compassion wherever it leads and whatever it costs in the life of this institution, so that in a world of harsh tensions, deep misunderstandings, much blindness, and spiritual insensitivity, he and Wabash College together might continue to grow and prosper by simply shining in the darkness and lighting the path of life to all who pass this way. Amen.

Invocation at Installation Luncheon for Dr. Frederick Seitz, Rockefeller University President
October 8, 1968

We pray today especially for your blessings upon Dr. Frederick Seitz that, through him and his vital leadership, this university may continue to grow and to prosper. Grant him the fullness of the virtues he will need in the days ahead: The *wisdom* to know the difference between what is important and what is irrelevant in the life of this university; the *patience* to listen and the *courage* to act, the *humility* to know what even he cannot do—and the list is long for every university president—the *grace* to make of this university an ever more human and humane community wherein everyone, high and low, shares the ideals of this place and partakes of the real joy of discovery and intellectual accomplishment. Wisdom, patience, courage, humility, grace—may all of these be his in abundance, but, above all, Lord, grant him the great gifts that redeem the university and our times today, the gifts of love and laughter: for the old have too often forgotten how to love and the young how to laugh. If the world is too cold and too serious today, may this new leader create here a fellowship of young and old who can lighten the burdens of the day by love and brighten the day itself by laughter, for we are in your hands, O Lord, and without your help we do all too little, but we do share your love and are at peace in your joy. Amen.

Homily Delivered at Opening of School Year
September 11, 1977

. . . We begin again in prayer and confidence—perhaps better said, confident because we pray.

To whom do we pray? Each one of you must speak for yourself, but I am willing to expose myself, as perhaps I should, standing here before so many colleagues whose lives, like my own, have been so intimately linked over so many years in this noble endeavor called Catholic higher education.

To whom do we pray today? It is easiest just to say that we pray to God. For a child, it is easy to visualize an anthropomorphic Father, by which name God is most easily called, as indeed Jesus addressed him in the prayer he taught us. As we grow older and are introduced to the true wonder of the Christmas story, the splendor of God-made-man who dwelt among us, prayer comes quite congenially to address Jesus Christ, Our Lord and Savior, whose birth brought divinity visibly among us, whose life and the good news he proclaimed touches our lives at so many focal points, whose suffering, death, and resurrection, daily commemorated in the Holy Mass, give redemptive meaning to our suffering and death and the hope of ultimate resurrection to eternal life. "I am the way, the truth and the life. . . . Who lives and believes in Me has eternal life and I will raise him up on the last day."

In my own life, as I grew older still, there came a further Trinitarian progression to prayer and the God whom we so falteringly address. God is not only Father and Son, but the Holy Spirit as well. The sweep of revelation from Genesis, "Let there be light," to John's "And the word became flesh and dwelt among us, full of grace and truth, and of His fullness we have all received" did not end there. Over the years, I have been increasingly seized by the intimate words of Jesus to his beloved few, the night before he died. Let me repeat a few of those words from John's account of the Last Supper:

> My little children, I will not be with you much longer. I give you a new commandment: Love one another, just as I have loved you, you must love one another. By this love you have for one another, everyone will know that you are My disciples. (13:33–35)
>
> Do not let your hearts be troubled. Trust in God still and trust in Me. (14:1)
>
> Whatever you ask for in My name, I will do it. . . . I shall ask the Father and He will give you another Advocate, to be with you forever, the Spirit of Truth, whom the world can never receive since it neither sees nor knows Him; but you know Him, because He is with you, He is in you. I will not leave you orphans. (14:13–18)
>
> I have said these words to you, while still with you; but the Advocate, the Holy Spirit, whom the Father will send in My name, *will teach you everything and remind you of all I have said to you.* (14:25–26)

Christmas is ever heartwarming and tender. Easter is full of joy and hope. But at Pentecost, Christianity really began in earnest. Poor, inadequate men and women, adrift and afraid and seemingly hopeless, suddenly received the fire of the Holy

Spirit and went out to cast the fire of the good news all across the world. Until today, when over a billion men and women call themselves Christians.

It is not my point this morning to trace the work of the Spirit over these two millennia from Pentecost until now, but to emphasize that the Christian work that brings all of us together, at this time and in this place, is indeed a preeminent work of the Spirit. I might also add that those of us whose whole lives are given to the work of education might best pray today to the Holy Spirit, for the gifts he gives are those we need most for the success of our work. I will only mention the two gifts for which I pray most often, for myself and for each of you.

First, wisdom. The first time that I preached on this occasion, for the 111th school year beginning in 1952, I preached on education and wisdom. I seek wisdom no less today. Throughout scripture, wisdom is imaged as light. Even Our Lord said, "I am the Light of the world," and St. John says "that [His] life was the light of men, a light that shines in the darkness, a light that darkness could not overpower" (Jn 1:4–5).

Our most basic task as educators in a world of darkness is to be bearers of the light of truth and wisdom. We and our students live in a world of darkness where physical and material power is mainly cherished: In the macro-world, the power of wealth, the power of military might, the power of political clout, the power of vast communication empires, the power of enormous industrial enterprises. In the micro-world, the power of the atom, DNA, the gene, the virus, the neutron, the thermo-nuclear reaction. None of these powers is evil of itself, only in its use, which often enough through human malevolence contributes to the power of darkness.

Against all of this physical power, we say to our students, I hope we do, that there is a primacy of the spiritual, that action is both useless and dangerous without prior thought, that the greater the physical power available, the greater the need for spiritual values that must control its use. Man cannot live humanly or even survive in a world of darkness without the light of wisdom. Those of us who presume to teach young people to live and cope in such a world of wild and unruly and enticing power must most of all be endowed with the wisdom that orders all knowledge and power toward the good of mankind, peace, and the glory of God, too.

No one has to argue to this assembly that the university is and must increasingly be the house of the intellect. But we do humbly pray today that our intellects are not merely filled with knowledge, for knowledge without wisdom can lead to blind pride and darkness. We were recently led into a dark abyss in Vietnam by the best and the brightest, who were competent and learned, but not wise.

We pray to be wise men and women who see a wholeness and an order and a meaning to life and to humanity's total quest for light in the surrounding darkness. We pray to be modest and humble about what we know because there is so much that we do not know, so much that only faith can illuminate. We also pray to be wise in time, so that one day we might enjoy, and lead others to enjoy, the light of God's vision in eternity, for without the promise of eternal life, this life can be a cruel hoax, a mad tragedy.

Wisdom makes the difference. There is a marvelous description of wisdom in the Old Testament's Book of Wisdom: "She is a breath of the Power of God, pure emanation of the glory of the Almighty. . . . She is a reflection of the eternal light, untarnished mirror of God's active power, image of His goodness. . . . She makes all things new. In each generation, she passes into holy souls, she makes them friends of God and prophets, for God loves only the man who lives with wisdom" (7:25–27).

Negatively, Wisdom says, "Wretched are those who scorn wisdom and disciplines: their hope is void, their toil unavailing, their achievements unprofitable" (3:11).

Let us pray today that wisdom may be the fulfillment of our learning, the substance of our teaching, the light of our lives in this Seat of Wisdom, which is another name of Notre Dame, Our Lady.

The second gift of the Holy Spirit that I would like to pray for today is courage. This may seem a somewhat pedestrian request after wisdom, but I think not. Why do educators need courage, especially today? First, because there is so much counterfeit education going on today, both formally and informally, that it takes a courageous person to stand firm and breast the rising tide of pragmatism, incompetence, foolishness, and valuelessness that is, all around us, passing for education.

Too many educators are afraid to say that whatever we teach students to do, it is even more important to teach them what kind of persons they should be. This means that they must be taught values as well as skills, and we must teach the values by courageously exemplifying them. It takes courage to say that there is no easy path to truth, and competence, and wisdom, and that each of these is far more important than false but easy victories, moral ambiguity or neutrality, and cunning deceit in life. Robert Hutchins in 1935 courageously told his graduates: "Believe me, you are closer to the truth now than you will ever be again. Do not let 'practical' men tell you that you should surrender your ideals because they are impractical. Do not be reconciled to dishonesty, indecency, and brutality because gentlemanly ways have been discovered to be dishonest, indecent, and brutal. . . . Courage, temperance, liberality, honor, justice, wisdom, reason and understanding, these are still the virtues." He added thirty years later: "The life of man, so far as it is of value at all, is at every point a struggle of wisdom against folly, of generosity against selfishness, of objectivity against prejudice, of civilization against barbarism."

In a world where so few of us can glory in freedom, it takes courage to use our freedom to promote justice, even when justice is unpopular; to reject falsehood when everyone else says that the naked emperor is well clothed; to unmask the shoddy, the superficial, and the ersatz when others are applauding it because it happens to be in vogue.

Courage is most important for educators because courage makes our inner integrity viable and our students learn integrity best when they see us practice it courageously. Courage brings wisdom out of our inner being and makes it visible in the way we judge life's options and how faithfully we follow those paths that we judge best, even though difficult. Every good value we hold requires steadfast courage, so does every good initiative, every faithful act, every generous deed.

I spent a week at Aspen last month leading an Executive Seminar on the Nature of Man. After sampling the classical Chinese, Greek, Roman, Medieval, Renaissance and modern texts, after more than twenty hours of discussion, one strong conviction, an old one for me, came through to all with startling clarity—whatever one thinks of man's and woman's potential goodness, there is something more that we all desperately need to be good: the enlightenment of wisdom and the strength of courage, both born of faith and prayer.

It is in that faith and with that prayer that I call upon the Holy Spirit today, as we begin once again with hope and joy and confidence to take part together in this noble and creative work that we call education. May the Holy Spirit grant us all wisdom and courage, the light to see and the strength to do, and may he likewise illuminate and strengthen our students, too. I conclude with an English version of my favorite Pentecostal hymn, *Veni Sancte Spiritus*, "Come, Holy Spirit," ascribed to Stephen Langton, who was born in the year 1150 and died in 1228.

> Holy Spirit, God of light,
> Fill us with Your radiance bright;
> Gentle father of the poor,
> Make us, by Your help, secure;
> Come, Your boundless grace impart,
> Bring Your love to ev'ry heart.
> Lord of consolation, come,

Warm us when our hearts are numb;
Great consoler, come and heal,
To our souls Your strength reveal;
Cool, refreshing comfort pour,
And our peace of mind restore.
Light immortal, fire divine,
With Your love our hearts refine;
Come, our inmost being fill,
Make us all to do Your will;
Goodness You alone can give,
Grant that in Your grace we live.
Come, our lukewarm hearts inspire,
Mold our wills to Your desire;
In our weakness make us strong,
And amend our every wrong;
Guide us when we go astray,
Wash our stain of guilt away.
Give to ev'ry faithful soul
Gifts of grace to make us whole;
Help us when we come to die,
So that we may live on high;
Ever let Your love descend,
Give us joys that never end.

PART V

LIVES OF LEARNING

> Grant us first and most of all wisdom, so that
> we may ever see the whole of life and of learn-
> ing, in its total comprehensive beauty, and not
> be blinded by a myopic preoccupation with one
> of its parts, or with some particular problem of
> this passing hour, or swayed unduly by our inner,
> unspoken pride, prejudice, passion, or pettiness.
> —*Fr. Ted Hesburgh, CSC*

Perhaps the topic of learning appears tangential in a collection
of spiritual writings, but for Fr. Ted, faith and learning remain
inextricably linked. He took his vocation as an educator as seriously as his calling to the priesthood, seeing these ministries
as a singular calling which God was asking him to undertake.
Perhaps for this reason he turned down invitations to leave education for other roles, such as that of a prelate or government
official. Fr. Ted believed that God, the omniscient Creator, is
visible in all creation, and therefore all forms of knowledge could
eventually lead back to the God of all rationality and understanding. Formed in the image of God and in need of God's
mercy, humanity is given an inherent curiosity to examine and
discover the world around them. This enables the faithful to seek
the Spirit's guidance in comprehending, stewarding, and communicating about Creation. In a world eager to sever education
from any religious ties, it is crucial for individual learners and

for institutions of learning to recognize God as the source of all truth and goodness.

This section fittingly begins with invocations in which Fr. Ted asks God for those virtues most essential to true education, recognizing the divine hand behind the wondrous handiwork of Creation. Also included in this section are several sermons that open the school years by returning teaching and learning to an eternal perspective: "doing all we might do to redeem and reorder and revive the world in which we live today." Addressing outspoken critics of this purposeful Church role in education, Fr. Ted articulated the Christian university's responsibility in exposing error and evil and in facilitating reconciliation between humanity and its Maker, rejecting moral ambiguity for faithful, sacred certainty.

Invocation
No Date

O Lord God, Father, Guide, and Guardian of us all, we ask thee this day to send thy Holy Spirit upon us, to grant us the virtues that our profession demands and that our times require. Grant us first and most of all *wisdom*, so that we may ever see the whole of life and of learning, in its total comprehensive beauty, and not be blinded by a myopic preoccupation with one of its parts, or with some particular problem of this passing hour, or swayed unduly by our inner, unspoken pride, prejudice, passion, or pettiness. Grant us also *prudence*, so that we may choose the proper and fitting means to achieve our exalted purposes in education; keep us from confusing means and ends; help us to realize that we can compromise on means, but never on our ultimate goals the pursuit of excellence in all we do. Grant us, Lord, a deep sense of *understanding* and *compassion*, for our students, first of all, for without them our profession would lack purpose and meaning; then grant us understanding and compassion for our fellow workers on whatever level of education, and from whatever institution. Help us see that only understanding and compassion can keep us working together and not at cross purposes. Grant us too, O Lord, some new infusion of the *enthusiasm, idealism, and energy* that characterized our youth, that we may not grow stodgy, pedestrian, uninspired and uninspiring in our later years. You know, Lord, that we have ample reason to be tired and discouraged at times, but keep the inner purpose and dedication of our lives as educators, as those fortunate few entrusted with the minds and hearts of American youth, keep this goal shining and bright within us, and let it, at least once in a while, shine forth in our eyes, in our actions, and in our lives. Grant us lastly, O Lord, the kind of *courage* that leads when leadership is most difficult and most needed. Grant us the courage to follow our convictions to the end of the road, not just to the first easy stop along the way. Grant us the courage to speak loudly and clearly, unmistakably for all in the nation to hear, declaring what is wise, and just, and true, and good in our times and for our people, even when they do not want to hear what we have to say. Lord, there are not many things that we ask of thee: wisdom, prudence, understanding, compassion, enthusiasm, idealism, energy, and courage. We do believe that they are important virtues for all of us though, perhaps spelling out by their presence or absence in our lives, whether we are faithful or unfaithful servants, good or poor educators. While we pray for these virtues, Lord, grant that we may ever cherish them and work with them until the day is ended and night falls upon our lives. Then, in thy mercy, grant us for our labors and by thy grace, a place of refreshment and light, and peace at last: the blessed vision of thyself, through Christ Our Lord, Amen.

Invocation Delivered at the Centennial of Engineering Luncheon
Chicago, September 10, 1952

Bless us, O Almighty God, Creator of heaven and earth, whose physics is the rainbow by day and the flash of lightning etched against the blackness of the night, whose mathematics are the stars, whose canvas is the bended heavens upon which thou dost paint the glory of the morning and of the evening sun. The miracle of the ripening grain is thine, who gives us this day our daily bread; the hidden chemistry in the heart of the earth is thine, which transforms the forests of an earlier day foregone into the coal and oil whose power has wrought the wonders of modern industry. Grant us to be humble under thy generous hand and to acknowledge that without thee we can do nothing, but can do all things in thee, who strengthens us. For thou hast made man a little less than the angels, thou hast crowned him with glory and honor, and hast placed him over all the works of thy hands.

Give us wisdom ever to be conscious of that stewardship, to live and labor for the betterment of man to the glory of thy name, and to merit at the last "a safe lodging and a holy rest" through Jesus Christ, Our Lord, Amen.

Statement on Spiritual Values in the Lives of Young Americans
August 12, 1953

An ever-increasing number of educators in America are becoming more concerned with the place and adequacy of religious education in our times. Perhaps this is a reaction to the secularism that has pervaded education generally in decades past. More substantially, this concern for religious education stems from the growing conviction that the spiritual values that highlighted the stirring documents of our Founding Fathers are even more important today if young Americans are to be prepared to carry to the world the God-given heritage of human dignity and freedom which our Founding Fathers brought to the birth of this nation. Indeed, our cherished American way of life is unintelligible apart from God and spiritual values. To divorce this precious heritage from its inner core, to infer by absolute neglect that religion has no place in American education, would be to deprive Americans of what has, from our earliest days, been typically American.

Our greatest American leaders have been humbly great to their common acknowledgment of God's blessings upon our land and our people. They have not been ashamed to ask for a continuation of these divine blessings, for they have realized that "Unless God keeps the city, they labor in vain to build it." . . .

Sermon for the Opening of the School Year
September 26, 1954

. . . The question might be rephrased and asked in more familiar form: Why have a great Catholic university, or any Catholic university at all? The only legitimate answer would have to demonstrate that a Catholic university has a function, as university and precisely as Catholic, fulfilled by no other. This function would have to meet a real and vital need in the world today, a need being met by no other agent. All other universities would suffer by comparison to such a providential institution. This institution would be proud of its place in the world, would fulfill its mission with enthusiastic zeal and unrelenting effort. . . .

Universities, like all other human institutions, came into being because men saw in them an answer to a crying human need. Of course, these needs vary somewhat from age to age. This results in a varied emphasis on the part of the university. This much thought, I think, should be stated as a matter of stable principle regarding university objectives, irrespective of the actual cultural, political, religious, or economic climate of any age: The university is by its essential nature committed to the mission of learning and teaching. The university is born when human minds are at work together for intellectual purposes. The university prospers when men are willing to stand firmly for the value of things intellectual, to devote themselves wholeheartedly to study and learning and teaching that the human intellect may "become richer and stronger, broader in appreciation and sympathy, more firm in judgement, more sure in action . . . to gain at last some measure of wisdom, some vision of truth, some understanding of the Will of God."

It was such a vision and such an intellectual human need that first drew men together in an association that became a university at Paris, Bologna, Louvain, Chartres, Oxford, and Cambridge. It might be noted that all these were Catholic universities too, since all their learning was ordered under the egis of theology, the highest wisdom. They were not called Catholic then, as there was nothing else comparable that would necessitate this qualification. They are not Catholic today because much has happened since, religiously, culturally, politically, and economically, to further complicate this essential intellectual task of the university. There is nothing we can do to change what has transpired since the founding of the first universities. But we can and must try to understand this historical background in its dynamism and general direction, because it has fashioned the world we live in today. Our particular task as a modern Catholic university is certainly more complicated than in medieval times. Yet, our work today is more challenging and certainly more vitally needed because of the climate in which we do live.

How do we summarize what has happened? The very listing of the historical figures brings to mind the strong currents of new theologies and new philosophies that made the ordered flow of knowledge a swirling, churning vortex of conflicting assertions and denials. Luther and Calvin, Francis Bacon, Descartes, and Rousseau, Hobbes, Locke, and Voltaire, Hume, Kant, and Hegel, Darwin, James, and Dewey. This is part of the genealogy.

It is equally difficult to summarize the kaleidoscopic nightmare of isms that have ebbed and flowed through these past four centuries: rationalism, skepticism, agnosticism and atheism; voluntarism, pragmatism, dialectic materialism, and existentialism; positivism, scientism, mechanism, and relativism. However good the intentions, however valid the critical spirit, however sincere the authors, one cannot view the actual results we have inherited today without shuddering at the formidable task of putting all the pieces back into order again. Nothing has escaped this intellectual disorder—neither man in his spirit, his mind, and his will; not society, government, history, or law; not the world itself, nor God who made it. All are denied, *de-natured, de-spiritualized.* And as a somber closing note, we find a growing distrust of intellectuals and things intellectual by those who should ordinarily look to great minds for leadership.

One ray of light, one road of hope remains. Minds have created this disorder and minds alone can begin to remake the order that has largely been lost. It was for this purpose that God gave us our minds—that there might be order and ordered growth in man and in his world. It was for this purpose that the medieval universities were founded—to further the acquisition of those intellectual virtues of understanding, wisdom, science, prudence, and art. It was through such discipline of the mind that the first universities hoped to influence persons and society, to quench the thirst for truth in the minds of men, to enable the intelligence of man to order and dispose of human acts in the light of truth in all its fullness. This was a high calling at that time. It is an even higher calling today, given the need of our times for what we alone as a Catholic University can offer: adequacy of knowledge, truth in all its fullness, human and divine.

A Protestant educator had to remind us recently that ours is the richest and most constant intellectual tradition in the Western world. What does this tradition say? It says that there is a God, Father, Son, and Holy Spirit. That he made all that is and man particularly after his image and likeness: with spiritual endowments of intelligence and free will, and an eternal destiny of perfect happiness with God. It says that man is fallen, but not totally corrupted, that Adam's fall was a kind of felicitous error since the Son of God became man in the person of Jesus Christ. That Christ lived and died to redeem us, and founded an age-long Mystical Body to continue his work of incarnation and redemption, to teach, govern, and sanctify all men in Christ. That men are persons, free and equal as sons of God and brothers of Christ, endowed with dignity and called to greatness. This tradition prizes the power of man's mind in all of its search for truth and the expression of truth through science, art, philosophy, and, most highly, through theology, wherein man is given a direct assist in his quest for truth through God's own revelation.

This tradition prizes the freedom of man, not as absolute, but as a power to choose what is best, even the divine. This tradition cherishes and promotes the inviolability of man's rights as a person, seeks justice and charity, law and order, truth, the good and the beautiful. The century-long tradition of Christian wisdom seeks all of these things in order and symmetry, in peace and understanding, and would have them produce a profound and rich Christian culture today, even as in the latter dark ages it disciplined minds and souls and drew men from barbarism into a world of natural and supernatural reality. This tradition is the same one that created legal institutions when the Western world was in transition from barbarism to civilization; this tradition fostered the arts, preserved the documents, founded the schools and universities, and taught men that they could know, love, and serve God while transfiguring the natural world by the intelligence and freedom and creativity that are in man's nature because he is made in God's image.

If we have been at times unmindful of this tradition, how could we have forgotten the great persons who made it live and grow in their day? Athanasius, Leo, Augustine, Ambrose, Gregory, Bede, Bernard, Albert, Aquinas, Bonaventure, all intellectual giants, and holy men, too, for as Rabanus Maurus said, no one can perfectly achieve wisdom unless he loves God. Then there were the great creative geniuses in literature and the arts: Dante, Chaucer, Fra Angelico, Michelangelo, Da Vinci, Thomas More, Palestrina, Pascal. Science has had its share and more: Copernicus, Galileo, Linacre, Lavoisier, Pasteur, Mendel, even our own Nieuwland.

How, one might ask, could the intellectual climate of the Western world have become so clouded if such is the strong tradition of such valiant men? Perhaps the answer to this question may hurt, but it should be faced. The tradition of Christian wisdom was more vital centuries ago than it is today. The great Catholic scholars were more plentiful in the past than they are in the present. Why? I fear that the dynamic and creative forces behind the movement were dissipated by the turn of events and became less vital. Christian philosophy spent itself in dialectics and sterile distinctions, did not keep pace with an awakening of scientific curiosity and method. Catholic theology repeated itself into formalistic patterns that were more mindful of the enemy than the eternal spring of new Christian life and wisdom within. We defended the walls, but we ceased to build the city, and we looked too seldom to the new problems beyond the walls in the new secularistic city of man.

All this may be explained away by saying that at least we still live and still do have schools and universities—but again comes the agonizing inquiry: Are we really doing all we might do to redeem and reorder and revive the world in which we live today?

I grant that it is easy to condemn the past. Our own American past gives us much to be thankful for. Notre Dame's own history is a thrilling account of sacrifice, devotion, and sheer pioneering doggedness that brought this University from a low grade grammar school to what it is today.

But the present and the future are our immediate problem as we begin the 113th year in Notre Dame's history. I would say to you today that the pioneering days of childhood and youth are over. And if we are staggered to think of the Herculean tasks already performed in childhood and youth, I would further stagger you with the thought that to be true to our vital mission, even more prodigious tasks are ahead to achieve maturity.

I would apply to ourselves today the fullness of the words of two great men, Leo XIII and Bishop Spaulding regarding universities.

Leo XIII wrote: "The end of the Catholic university forever will be this: with the light of Catholic truth showing the way to provide for youth in our country the *fullness* and the *best* of learning on the highest levels."

And Bishop Spaulding:

> A true university will be the home of ancient wisdom
> and new learning; it will teach the best that is known

and encourage research; it will stimulate thought, refine taste, and awaken a love of excellence; it will be at once a scientific institute, a school of culture and a training ground in the business of life; it will educate the minds that give direction to the age, it will be the nursery of ideas, a center of influence . . . that which is the strongest in man is mind, and when a mind truly vigorous, open, supple and illuminated reveals itself, we follow in its path of light.

Here is no physical task of survival in a raw new land. Here is a demanding spiritual task of the highest order, in fullest accord with the rich age-old tradition of Christian wisdom. Here is an apostolate that no secular university today can undertake—for they are largely cut off from the tradition of adequate knowledge which comes only through faith in the mind and faith in God, the highest wisdom of Christian philosophy and Catholic theology.

Here is a task that requires that we be conscious of our past heritage, and enthusiastic in bringing new insights of Christian wisdom to the present. Here is a task for the greatest minds, and the most devoted hearts and completely dedicated lives.

I know of no other spot on earth where we might make a better beginning than here at Notre Dame, where we might inaugurate a new center of Christian culture to effect a reawakening of the potential of Christian wisdom applied to the problems of our age.

This is no work of defense, no declaration of war, no practice in isolation, but a move to revitalize our own understanding of the treasure of supreme intellectualism and divine faith, wedded in strength and beauty. It means working together, each with our own particular talents to exploit the full power of Christian wisdom to order what is disordered, to complete what is good but incomplete, to meet insufficient knowledge with the fullness of truth, to give a new direction and a wider, saner perspective to all that is good and true in our times.

The time is ripe. The old errors are sunk in frustration and pessimism and disorder. Men of goodwill are not wanting. Darkness awaits a light. We have done and are doing a wide variety of good things at Notre Dame. If we do everything else and fail in this, our proper task, our high calling, our providential mission, then as we pray in the presence of God here today, we will be unworthy servants, and a failure as a Catholic university.

Let us pray then, sincerely and humbly this morning, as we begin another academic year. Let us ask again and again for wisdom and courage, the light to see and the strength to do what the times demand and the richness of our heritage promises.

Sermon for the Opening of the School Year
September 25, 1955

If you continue in My word, you shall be
My disciples indeed. And you shall know the
truth, and the truth shall make you free.
—*Jn 8:31–32*

At the beginning of each school year, we pause for a solemn moment of prayer: that God may bless our common endeavor of the months to come, and that he may also confirm each of us in our dedication to this lofty endeavor that demands the best that is in each of us.

We also pause for a few moments this morning to consider some aspect of the work at hand, to glean, if possible, some added inspiration from the thought that ours is no common task, no ordinary calling.

This year, I shall try to review what might be termed the social challenge of the educative process. Social development is not the primary purpose of education, but neither is it an unimportant by-product. Education is primarily concerned with an individual person. We attempt as teachers to draw to some fulfillment the inner powers of the person: his capacity for discerning truth, his yearning for the inner freedom which is nurtured by the growing possession of truth, integrated knowledge and ultimately wisdom which gives meaning and conscious order to all that is known. Education must further and, more indirectly, be a school of love, for truth and beauty and the good things of life are not merely to be known, but to be assimilated in the person who is made to possess by love as well as to see by knowledge.

Education and the work of educators could cease at this point, if the person educated could live his life in solitary contemplation and love. But the student, like ourselves, is living in an historic moment of time, in a real world with all its actual tensions and current crises. The university cannot abstract itself or its students from the realities of past history or the anguish of the present crisis. Even if the university accomplishes its primary mission in relative geographic seclusion from the intemperate cross currents of the forum and the marketplace, it cannot shelter itself or its students from the conflict of ideas that are the most real substratum of these cross currents.

These ideas are engaged today in mortal conflict, and at the center of the struggle what is really at stake is the soul of man, his dignity, the truth by which alone he can live, his freedom to be what he was created to be. This man, whose soul and dignity and freedom are at stake, is the same man who is being educated. If in the process, he is not equipped to recognize the conflict of his times, to discern its basic issues, and to accept what part he must play to aid in final victory, then the university is indeed a parasite in a society that looks to it for leadership, and knowledge, for wisdom and integrity, at least in the minds and hearts of its graduates.

The first pages of recorded human history tell the story of conflict: good against evil, truth against falsehood, order against anarchy, obedience against pride, spirit against matter. It was not a story of victory then, nor is it a story of victory today in the worldwide present-day version of the original episode in the Garden of Eden. There have been classical victories and classical defeats in the age-old struggle and the battle lines have been extended and complicated in the intervening centuries.

What perhaps somewhat simplifies the picture today is that at least in the realm of basic ideology the battle line is clearly drawn. We can speak of the free world where the dominant social structures try to respect what is most sacred in Western culture: the dignity of man, his basic rights and freedoms, his inner aspirations for what is called the pursuit of happiness—the good life in a good society. And we can speak of the other half a world, where this concept of man does not obtain and is not respected.

Between these two worlds there is, and must be, real conflict. The terms of the conflict may change from year to year: now cold war, now lukewarm war, now again war disguised as peaceful coexistence. Yet, whatever the actual terms of the conflict, conflict it is, and conflict it will be as long as the soul of man is at stake, and the power of evil is at large.

There are many illusory solutions offered to end the present conflict: diplomatic moves and counter moves, the implied threat of more numerous and more destructive nuclear weapons, the full-fledged chicanery of every means of modern propaganda to strengthen one's position and to weaken that of the enemy. These and other solutions are illusory, because they fail to recognize that the conflict is not basically military, political, or economic. At heart, the conflict is both philosophical and theological. The actual battlefield is in the realm of ideas. No matter what the physical or material forces involved, ultimately it is ideas that will prevail, truth that will gain or lose in this struggle for the souls of men.

How does all of this affect the university and its mission of educating students in this year which we officially begin today? Obviously, we must have true and good ideas ourselves if we are to teach our students with conviction and inspire them to hunger, to search for, to find and to embrace the truth. For it is only the truth ultimately that will make us truly free.

How is the truth represented today on our side of the crucial struggle? We are so often oratorically critical of the opposition that the obvious assumption is that he is all wrong and that we are all right. But in a more reflective mood, might we not ask how right we really are, or to put it another way, if we are right, are we right for the right reasons? Our assessment of this situation will mightily affect the attitudes that are reflected in our educational process.

No one in the West would seriously question the fundamental truth of the democratic charter. But too few of us question the present-day vitality of its tap roots: the soul of Christianity and Western culture from which it laboriously grew. The opposition at least is clear about its precedents: Communism is the product of naturalism and materialism full blown. The Communist clearly recognizes totalitarianism as an end in itself to be furthered by any means. Perhaps because of its more recent origin, the Communist sees more clearly the logical and vital connection between his philosophy and its conclusions in the practical order of social life.

But how many in the West would recognize that democracy, unlike the totalitarian scheme, is not an end in itself—but a temporal means of preserving the ultimate human values of a spiritual order: the dignity of man, his rights and responsibilities to his fellow men under God, his inner spiritual freedom to seek a personal destiny that transcends temporal society. These spiritual values can be achieved by means of a democratic society. They may also exist, to some extent, without the precise political order that we have, but democracy, as we know it, cannot exist without these spiritual values. The inner contradiction of our day is simply this: that we have accepted the democratic charter, enjoyed a great and wonderful gift of ages past, a gift flowing from the inner dynamism of Christianity and from a deep dedication to the value of the spirit in man, and then, having accepted the fruit, we have forgotten the root and branch. We have, in large measure, allowed the soul of our culture to die, while living on the rich, but rapidly diminishing, heritage of the past.

This is what Plato long ago condemned as "living by habit without fixed principle." Ours is the house now resting on sand about which Our Lord warned us. The fair day has passed; the winds and the rains have come. We must now look to the foundations of our social order. It is no longer enough to accept conclusions and to abdicate the principles which alone can validate the conclusions.

How popular, or even acceptable, in present day university circles are the vital philosophical principles, the living Christian faith that gave birth to the democratic charter after ages of tyranny and human oppression? Most universities teach everything but theology, the science of faith. The philosophy in vogue is strangely akin to that naturalism and materialism that the opposition so logically pursues.

Glance for a moment at these philosophies. Naturalism denies outright man's relation both to an ultimate order of values and to God who is the source of these absolutes. Naturalism thus divorces man from the spiritual and moral order to which he belongs and without which he will be destitute of any reasonable order or direction in life. Standing all alone, endowed with perfectibility by courtesy of Rousseau, man is left without any norm or sanction beyond himself and his own desires, individual when he can press them, and collective when they are pressed upon him. The natural result is pride and egotism. All man has left to worship or serve is himself or his false gods of money or power, nation or race.

At this point, try to see the logic of those educators in our day who in practice try to preserve the dignity of man while intellectually subscribing to a basically materialistic philosophy that recognizes man as little more than a highly developed animal, on earth. And where is the logic of still enjoying a democratic charter, derived from belief in absolute spiritual and moral values, long after these same basic values have been discarded from the educational process as unsophisticated or archaic or, what is most devastating today, unscientific.

We might have lingered longer in this sorry state of intellectual schizophrenia had not the present crisis developed. Perhaps in the Providence of God, Communism will do this service to the world, and especially to us of the Western world, to demonstrate in its starkest reality the logical consequences in the social order of a fully conscious naturalistic and materialistic concept of man and his destiny.

We are no longer concerned in the West today with a more or less perfect democratic charter, but with the life or death of this idea and its reality in the face of a fiercely competitive idea and reality that will have all the world or nothing. This is no high school debate, but a life and death struggle with naturalism and materialism on the march, inflamed with pride and passion and zeal, armed with an apocalyptic drive, vast political power, clever propaganda, and the vision of world domination.

Against this force shall we oppose a democratic charter that is unsure of its presuppositions, robbed of the strength it once drew from vital dynamic principles. Shall we dare to hope for victory if we have thrown away our arms—the sword of the spirit, the might of the Lord of Hosts, the force of vital ideas, the courageous traditions of men who believed, and hoped and loved—that truth might prevail and that man, under God, might be truly free to live his life and to achieve his destiny in a social order based on absolute justice and law.

The basic social problem of the West would still be with us tomorrow if Communism were obliterated today. Without the pressure of Communism, we would not be more strong, only less harassed. The inner dynamism of the democratic charter would still need strengthening to survive, even if it were alone in this world. Death comes to a culture or a civilization, not solely from external pressures, but, even more often, from the inner withering of a vital principle, from a loss of faith, from moral anemia, and from the abdication of a basic commitment to truth and integrity. Yes, even without the threat of Communism, we would still be obliged to revitalize our faith, to revivify basic respect for our philosophical roots, not because they are useful or helpful to us in this conflict, but because they are true.

Here then, in the realm of truth, is the mission of the university manifest. If our graduates are to have a vital part in the struggle for men's souls, they must begin by achieving true wisdom and freedom in their own souls. This inner development may seem distant from the dramatic issues of Washington, Moscow, and Geneva. But the action that takes place in those distant scenes is the result of ideas that began their existence in the minds of men like Machiavelli, Kant, Rousseau, Hegel, Hobbes, Marx, Engels, Lenin, and Stalin on the one hand, and, on the other, ideas that burgeoned in the minds of Plato, Aristotle, Augustine and Aquinas, Madison and Jefferson, Washington and Lincoln. Throughout the ideas of the latter, there is the ever-present leaven of the divine ideas of Christ and the accumulated wisdom of Western thought on the dignity of man, his inalienable rights, his responsibilities to God and his fellow men, justice, law, and equity.

A university today will have an impact on the progress of man and human society, in direct proportion to the truth of the heritage it imparts to its students.

I would only like to signal today two of these basic truths that highlight the current conflict of ideas in the social order. They are likewise truths that traditionally have formed the cornerstone at Notre Dame, for an education productive of responsible leadership in the social order.

The first and most fundamental truth is the existence of one supreme, personal God, above and beyond history, infinite in knowledge and power, the Creator and Preserver of all that is, the Reality upon whom all that is, including man, depends, the beginning and the end. One God in Three Divine Persons, Father of whom we are called to be sons, Son Incarnate of whom we are brothers, Holy Spirit, the source of our highest inspiration for truth and love. The antithesis of this idea is atheism—the cornerstone of the opposition, the one basic reason that Communism is evil. No God, no creation, no providence, no spiritual reality, no freedom for good or evil, no ultimate beyond time, no higher norm for law, no eternal sanction for justice, no real basis for charity, no glimmer of immortality, no rights that are inalienable, no dedication that is divine, no order beyond nature, no meaning beyond matter. Here is the opposition to ideas that brooks no compromise. You are for God or against him. He is the center of human life or man is his own center. If God has spoken, if he has established an economy of salvation, then this is the all-important truth. Man can deny reality, truth, the good—but then he must create his own substitutes for these realities. And then he must live with his substitutes, and ultimately reality, truth, and the good will emerge to answer the anguished cry of a miserable humanity that pays the awful price of this denial.

Second, there is the truth of man, made in the image and likeness of God, made to glory in truth, made to love what is good and to enjoy beauty. Not the self-sufficient man of the naturalists, not the earthbound man of the materialists, but man who possesses dignity and immortality as a son of God and brother of Christ, man with all the inalienable rights he needs to act humanly, man fallen and yet redeemed, man endowed with divine life in his spirit through the grace of Christ, man who is a microcosm of the whole created universe, man whose spirit is free to range the universe, to love God and all else in God, man who shares the passion of Christ and the triumph of the risen Christ. And then there is the man of the Communists: akin only to the animals in his body, slave of the state, knowing only what can be seen and felt and sensed, determined by blind economic force, made to believe that anarchy is order, force is freedom, error is truth, and slavery is liberation. Man with no hope beyond bread and the reign of the proletariat under the Commissars, man not a little less than the angels, but just a little above the beasts.

Here again is an uncompromising conflict of ideas. We are either on one side, or on the other. Armies may wage war, diplomats may parlay, boundaries may be shifted, but in the end it is the idea that will win or lose. And it is only the truth that will set men free.

We might have lived in a different age, or not at all. We might have engaged ourselves in work of less significance or importance than education. But, in the Providence of God, we live today. We are engaged in this work, and the only important question to ask ourselves is this: Are we equal to the historical moment we face? Can we find within ourselves that burning commitment to the truth of God and his revelation, the consecration to the truth of man as we know him, and can we engender in a new generation of students a love of these basic truths, a commitment to what is good for man in the sight of God, a generosity to serve God and men for a resolution of the present conflict in modern society. We do not pray today that somehow all crises will miraculously cease, for crisis is the pattern of history and always will be. We only ask, humbly and confidently, that we may be worthy of the truth that is ours, for those on the side of truth are on the side of God and, ultimately, of victory. May Mary, Seat of Wisdom, guide us on our way this year.

Sermon for the Opening of the School Year
September 22, 1957

> At present, we are looking at a confused reflection in a mirror; then we shall see face to face; now, I have only glimpses of knowledge; then, I shall recognize God as He has recognized me.
> —*1 Cor 13:12*

As each new school year begins, it is my duty and my honor to appear before you and to highlight some of the things we pray for in this inaugural Mass of the Holy Spirit. If one would seek a common theme in my sermons of other years, it would be this:

that we are all committed here at Notre Dame to a common task of uncommon importance; that this task must somehow be doubly related, first, to the modern world in which we live, with all its tensions, its agonies, its new developments, and its vivid opportunities. Our task must likewise be related to that ancient wisdom that is ours to transmit, not by blind indoctrination, but with a vital sense of its relevance to the burning questions of our age. I have never said that ours is an easy task, and have indeed underlined some of the difficulties that complicate our activities. You will recall some of theses the explosive growth of knowledge that allows real competence in one field often at the expense of overall, integrated knowledge; then there is the intellectual atmosphere of secularism, an historical reality, that has resulted in a general disdain for theology and philosophy while seemingly more exciting windows of knowledge were and are being opened in other directions; then there has been our oftentimes poor and unenthusiastic comprehension of our own rich heritage, the bright light hidden under the bushel basket, the dull repetition of formulae and the all too frequent lack of burning dedication, enlightened curiosity, and hard unrelenting mental labor that alone can continue the ancient and worthy tradition of Catholic scholarship.

The particular problem that I wish to discuss with you this year is science, in the modern understanding of this word. I shall try to relate science and technology to some of the problems mentioned above. Science is the recognized darling of our day. Being a pragmatic people, we know it from its results—and these have been literally fantastic. Science has fed us, clothed us, housed us as man has never been fed or clothed or housed before. Science has cured a thousand ills, given clear sight to the myopic, hearing to the deaf. Science has prolonged our lives, speeded our communications, given us wings to lengthen our travels. Science has simplified our housekeeping, has given us amusement at the touch of a button. Science has indeed brought close the ends of the earth, and is now vaulting the space beyond.

Who will dare to say that these are not good things? No one need say this, but it should be said that there are other good and even better things if man does not live by bread alone. Science is most truly valued when it is viewed in the total perspective of man's life and destiny, not as an exclusive blessing. A well-fed, well-clothed, well-housed man can be ignorant, prejudiced, and immoral too. A healthy man can be as unjust as an unhealthy man. A long life is not necessarily good or fruitful. Vastly expanded communications devices do not guarantee that much worthwhile is being communicated, and a world brought close together is not necessarily a world at peace. Simplified house-keeping does not guarantee happy marriages; easily accessible amusement cannot banish the boredom of a pointless life; and vitamins are no substitute for virtues.

What I am saying is that there are many values that man has cherished, values that have ennobled him, and man stands to lose if he is seduced by the material benefits of science to the exclusion of the deep spiritual values that he cherished long before the advent of modern science and its accompanying tech-nology. We can say this, and still be grateful for the blessing of science. But there is much more to the problem than this initial and superficial comment, particularly when we relate the posi-tion of science in the modern world to the cognate problem of university education in a world that is so enamored of science and so indebted to it.

The task of the university today, viewed in relation to its students, is twofold. The university must somehow transmit the intellectual and moral treasures of the past to its students, and, in doing this, must also somehow integrate this heritage to the new perspectives of the present and the future. The first aspect of the task is easier than the second. It is possible merely to speak nostalgically of the past as if the present and its own real problems and opportunities did not exist. It is equally possible to live completely in the present, as in an isolation ward, with no perception of our past heritage, its values and vital human meaning. I suspect that many departments of many universities are doing just one or another of these incomplete tasks and, in so doing, are failing to educate truly.

What is this past that is so often referred to as the culture of the West? It is no simple reality, but an amalgam of many elements. The main currents of influence can be identified however. One finds at the base the great intellectual heritage that stems from the classical age of Greece. Here was the earliest root of the intellectual fiber of the West—the zest for universal understanding and philosophical inquiry, the joy of intellectual discovery, the deep values of things of the spirit: truth, beauty, and the good. The Romans added another dimension to the tapestry of the West, the ideal of law and order and a stable society of men with great civic institutions and an efficient administration of justice. Then there was the divine element of the Gospels, the fulfillment of the promise of the Old Testament, a new and bright light focused on man's nature and destiny, a fresh glimpse at the inner grandeur of the human person, new ideals of human thought, human achievement and high, indeed, eternal goals for human conduct. These three elements meshed to form what we know as Western culture. From this triple stock, we have derived that rich and complex heritage that is Western man's.

Whatever else man may become in the West in the years ahead, he will be poorer if, in his material progress, he loses the soul of this heritage which is centered in a concept of the human person as never fully understood before—glorying in the truth wherever and however it be found, strong and free under the law, cherishing art and beauty in its multitudinous forms, living by the highest spiritual ideals of the Gospel, dedicated to eternal values for which he is also ready to die, indeed, better to die than to lose them. Respect for all that is uniquely man's, spirit, mind, freedom, truth, justice, beauty—the inner dignity of the human person—this is the heritage of the West that is ours to have and to hold and to teach.

But this is not a static heritage: Truth can have new expression and fuller understanding; justice, new causes to champion; beauty, new forms to inspire. Somehow the university must re-comprehend, reinterpret, and reapply this heritage in every age. The heritage itself may become enriched and revitalized if this is done. If it is not done, the heritage may well become uninspiring, desiccated, devitalized, and even forgotten. Today science must be integrated as a part of this total heritage.

In a university context, the heritage is translated into many diverse disciplines: theology, philosophy, history, law, literature, language, economics, sociology, politics, mathematics, biology, physics, chemistry, geology, engineering. It is these latter, the physical sciences and their applications, that must be understood if they are to be integrated adequately into rich heritage that antedated the present explosive development of the physical sciences. I know not where this integration can take place if not in a university—where all knowledge is communicated and extended in its totality and, one might hope, in proper perspective.

The focus of the university task is perhaps best seen in what it attempts to achieve in the minds and hearts of its students. We have often said at Notre Dame that whatever else we do, we attempt to give all our students the basic elements of a liberal education: one that will liberate the young student from the bondage of ignorance, prejudice, and passion. Our basic endeavor in every undergraduate college is the development to excellence of the student's use of his intelligence and freedom. A liberal education should enable the young man to form a reasonably complete and accurate concept of God, the world, and man, some broad perception of man's situation and destiny in this world, and some inner realization of his relationship to God and to his fellow men. One would hope that all this would engender in the student some perspective and conviction so that the young man thus educated could direct his life in accordance with this total view of life's meaning. The really significant questions should be faced during this liberally educative process, the live options should be thoughtfully and even prayerfully considered, so that the maturing student is enabled to make, with an intelligence and freedom worthy of man, the important and difficult decisions that rational life demands. In summary, any education worthy of the riches of our Western culture, should somehow focus on the three great central realities of nature, man, and God.

It is certainly understandable how difficult this task of the university becomes in a world that is essentially secularistic and scientifically oriented in its forward march.

It need not be that the cultural values of man and the eternal importance of divine realities be lost or overshadowed in such a world. But such has been the direction of recent history: growing secularism, the divorce of the human from the divine, the temporal from the eternal, the material from the spiritual; and in the past century, the nineteenth-century scientists, in large numbers, declared that God and revelation and religion were now irrelevant.

At this present juncture of history, our greatest challenge and opportunity is to understand both the vital importance of our heritage and the growing importance of science, so that working together, instead of at cross purposes, our heritage may be enriched and science may become a fruitful instrument of man, not his master or destroyer. How can this be done?

Science can be a powerful adjunct to the process of liberal education that is at the heart of our mission, for science, too, is one of the liberal arts. No person can be liberally educated today without a reasonable grasp of science and the great new vision of the universe, in its innermost and outermost parts, that modern science has brought us. The scientific method can also bring new and imaginative and corrective insights into the educational process that was poorer without it. The student needs a respect for hard facts, accurately ascertained and expressed. Scientific curiosity, eagerness to postulate theoretical solutions and to verify them experimentally are worthy additions to mental maturity. Scientific speculation in the realms of pure science and mathematics prepares the student mentally for the more abstract studies of philosophy and theology which use intelligent reflection in another method of knowing to derive truths unattainable to physical science as such. Basic science and research may also engender in the student that respect for the mind at work which underlies all rational inquiry and human culture. Disrespect for the mind and the current sneering at intellectuals and intellectual endeavor is the quickest way to the destruction of all human culture. Scientific endeavor is finally a great school for discipline, for humility in the face of the yet unknown, for patience to work accurately, persistently, and painstakingly—all real virtues and values in the process of a liberal education.

Science needs the other academic disciplines, too, for there is more to human life than the understanding and manipulation of nature. Science is power, and power needs direction to be meaningful. It is man who is the scientist, and science exists in the world of man. This world has total perspectives and man has a destiny that goes beyond science. Science of itself cannot know God, or the nature of man; cannot establish justice, define morality, constitute culture, or write poetry.

In the university, however, all of these things can be done and students can learn all that is true and valid regarding God, man, and nature. The same student can see the broad sweep of revealed truth in theology, and the mind at work on ultimate problems in philosophy, too; he can glory in the intuitive insights of poetry, thrill at the recent discoveries of astrophysics, ponder the age-old lessons of human success and failure in history and literature. Perhaps the integration of all knowledge will somehow come to be in the mind of the student, but how, except accidently, if few of his professors really understand or appreciate each other's specialized branch of knowledge?

And how can all of the members of the academic community come to some basic understanding and appreciation of the totality of knowledge unless there is a continuing conversation among them on the points of contact between the various disciplines that make up the whole fabric of the universal knowledge?

I would not presume to outline such a conversation in its totality, but it might be helpful to illustrate its possible fruitfulness in one specific area most germane to what we have already been considering.

It is common knowledge that the theologians and the physicists have not been on speaking terms for centuries—so much so that they no longer speak the same language. Their falling out was a classic case of misunderstanding and, unfortunately, the Galileo incident is still regarded as a symbol of the presumed conflict between science and faith.

The climate has now begun to change—and on both sides. The time is ripe to take up a fruitful conversation left aside centuries ago. The lead article in the most recent issue of the best American Catholic theological journal was on "The origin and age of the universe appraised by science." Journals and bulletins of physicists have begun to carry challenging articles of philosophical and theological import. The physicists begin to sense a broader responsibility to the world of nuclear fusion and fission that they have introduced to the brink of great good or great evil. As America's most renowned physicist said after Hiroshima and Nagasaki—the scientist has now known sin, a theological reality.

Much could be gained, I believe, by frankly discussing the conflicts of the past. One might, without too much difficulty, defend the position that most of the conflict has resulted from bad theology and bad science, too.

The fundamental error at the beginning, in the case of Galileo, was that the proper theological questions were not asked. The real theological question involved was, how could this heliocentric doctrine of Copernicus and Galileo be squared with the fundamental Christian doctrine regarding the nature and destiny of man? Actually, there was and is no theological problem involved in the new theory. Instead of asking the proper theological question, however, the heliocentric system was viewed as opposed to

a literal interpretation of the early chapters of Genesis, an interpretation which one of the greatest theologians, St. Augustine,
would not have accepted centuries before Galileo, and which
certainly no scriptural theologian of note would sustain today.

Our present Holy Father, Pius XII, in a recent message to
the students of the Sorbonne clearly stated the case: "In your
studies and scientific research rest assured that no contradiction
is possible between certain truths of faith and established scientific facts. Nature, no less than revelation, proceeds from God
and God cannot contradict Himself. Do not be dismayed if you
hear the contrary affirmed insistently, even though research may
have to wait for centuries to find the solution of the apparent
opposition between science and faith."

Here in two brief phrases is the cause of most of the theolog-
ical-scientific disputes of the past: a misunderstanding of "the
certain truths of faith" and "established scientific facts." Too often
theologians have been all too little precise on what constitut-
ed "certain truths of faith." I say theologians, not the Church,
which has been consistent and unchanging in its precise official
statements of Catholic doctrine. And scientists, especially in the
last century, were overconfident, to put it mildly, about "established scientific facts." You are aware of the utterly materialistic
Victorian physicists who naively assumed the virtual finality,
immutability, and even literal truth of their description of the
nature of the world: the billiard ball models, Newton's laws of
motion and gravitation, Hooke's law of elastic strain, and all the
rest. Since then, we have seen centuries-old scientific views on
matter, space, and time summarily abandoned.

The latest theories are much more congenial to the corpus of
Christian theological doctrine. But let us suppose that present
scientific theories may again change in a way that may seem to
challenge theological truth. Should this possibility worry us? I
think not, and I have no fears from science. Truth is our knowledge of what is and, given a fundamental unity of all that is
and different valid ways of knowing it, the seeming conflicts

of today can merge into understanding tomorrow. Let us grant that there has been bad science and bad theology at times in the past. While the fundamental divinely revealed doctrines of the Church have never changed, theological understanding of them has progressed. Science, too, has progressed beyond false starts, and has learned to live with seemingly contradictory theories even within science itself—witness the history of scientific views on the theory of light. I am sure that theologians and physicists can live and work together fruitfully if they will only recognize the nature, the objectives, the limitations, and the methodological diversity of their different disciplines and share the quest along different paths for truth that is one. Science can learn things, such as the age of the earth, that theology as such cannot ever discover—given a lack of divine revelation on the subject. Theology, in turn, can know realities that are and always will be unknown to physical science as such: the notion of God and the good news of his economy of salvation for all the world and his promise of an eternal world to come.

Even Whitehead admitted that the notion of God was the greatest contribution of mediaeval theology to the formation of the scientific movement. You see, the theologian sees God not only as the Supreme Being of omnipotence and freedom, but also as the Source of rationality and order.

While God is free to create or not create a cosmos, and in choosing to create is free to create this cosmos or some other, when he did create this one, it was a cosmos, not a chaos, since it had to reflect his perfection and order. Because God is rational, his work is orderly, and because he is free, there is no predicting on our part as to just what this precise order will be. The world of Christian theism then is, at its foundation, a world congenial to empirical science with its twin method of observation and experiment. Unless there were regularities in this world, there would be nothing but chaos for science to discover, and because these are contingent regularities, they must be verified by experimentation.

One last word, and this one for the scientists. Who can measure the scientific effort and ingenuity that is expended on learning the few fragmentary scientific facts that we think we presently know for a certainty about the universe in its inner constitution and its outermost reaches? And yet, for the most part, scientists seem not too much concerned about the certain promise of divine revelation that for those who live and die in Christ, our Redeemer, there comes at the end of this earthly life the Blessed Vision of God himself and, in God, all things will be known eternally and, to the limit of our finite powers, comprehensively as in their cause. If this be true, and Catholics everywhere are prepared to die for its truth and promise, then at least it deserves some investigation. I make a point of this, for one of my good scientist friends recently wrote that he knew nothing of immortality and couldn't be less interested. Even as a friend, apart from being a priest, I felt sad that he was spending so much time and energy for such meager gain while completely missing the chance to attain eternally a universal knowledge that is so much greater and more lasting.

So much for a suggested conversation between the physicists and theologians and its possible fruitfulness toward the integration of knowledge. I return, in conclusion, to our original point of departure, something for which we might fruitfully pray at the beginning of this new academic year: that each one of us might cherish the task of seeking and imparting truth in every way possible; that we disdain no truth, be it theological, philosophical, historical, poetic, or scientific; that we ourselves may be examples of the kinds of minds and hearts, the kinds of human persons whom we try to fashion by the educative process; and that we try to appreciate all that is good in the past while we bring its wisdom to bear in directing and giving ultimate meaning to the powerful forces that are awakening in our world today. May God grant that this 115th year of our history will see us grow inwardly in wisdom, age, and grace, as we should, and may the university grow with us, as it most certainly will not grow without us.

Address at the Annual Meeting of the Council of Protestant Colleges and Universities
January 16, 1967

The Challenge Ahead

Everyone is likely to agree that the 817 Church-related colleges and universities in the United States face a future challenge. The only disagreement would be in the use of the word "future." Of course, equally great challenges face all the other private and public colleges and universities in this country. But our challenge is rather special, since it is encompassed in the broader challenge facing the Churches themselves in modern America, with or without the colleges and universities they sponsor. We who live and work in Christian colleges and universities not only face a challenge, we are already under fire, as are our Churches. One might best describe the challenge in its most dire terms as a challenge for survival. Those who predict our early demise do it about as discourteously as possible by saying that our institutions should never have been founded in the first place. Obviously then, for them, there is no point in continuing the farce. Even when it is granted that some of our institutions are among the top 10 percent in the nation academically, and are indeed admitted to be "America's unique contribution to higher education" (Cox, *Secular City*, 218), we are said to struggle daily "with what to do about a 'Church tradition' that usually seems less and less relevant to what they have to do to exist" (Cox, 219).

The critic I have been specifically quoting is Harvey Cox, although I could have just as well quoted an unhappy Catholic,

Dr. Rosemary Lauer, who says that the Church should get out of education. If you prefer someone from neither camp, we can fall back on George Bernard Shaw who said that a Catholic university is a contradiction in terms.

Cox is perhaps the most widely read of all the current critics, so let us first listen to his indictment in his own words:

> We have already noted that the university has always been a problem for the Church. But the current cleavage between the two is wider and more impassable than ever, precisely because we now stand at the end of the epoch of the Church's dominance in Western culture. (Cox, 219) . . .

> The anachronistic posture of the Church is nowhere more obvious than in the context of the university community. The Church has made three attempts to come to terms with the university problem in America, all of which have been marked by a certain recidivism. The first was the establishment of its own colleges and universities. This, of course, is medievalism. The whole idea of a *Christian* college or university after the breaking apart of the mediaeval synthesis has little meaning. The term Christian is not one that can be used to refer to universities any more than to observatories or laboratories. No one of the so-called Christian colleges that dot our Midwest is able to give a very plausible theological basis for retaining the equivocal phrase *Christian college* in the catalogue. Granted that there may be excellent traditional, public-relations, or sentimental reasons for calling a college Christian, there are no theological reasons. The fact that it was founded by ministers, that it has a certain number of Christians on the faculty or in the student body, that chapel is required (or not required), or that it gets part of its bills paid by a denomination—none of these factors provides any

> grounds for labeling an institution with a word that
> the Bible applies only to followers of Christ, and then,
> very sparingly. The idea of developing "Christian
> universities" in America was bankrupt even before
> it began. (Cox, 221)

I spare you the full flavor of his rhetoric on the other two means by which the Churches came to terms with the university problem in America. The second means was "residential congregations to render a special ministry to people involved in university life" (Cox, 221); the third was "to transplant onto the university campus a denominational Church disguised as a 'house' with ping-pong tables and a less ministerial minister" (Cox, 222). He adds later that "we are still in the third phase of this cumulative catastrophe." Apparently, we happy dinosaurs of the first unhappy phase are already written off and forgotten. Should we now curl up and die?

I do not want to vent my spleen criticizing Cox, word for word, as E. L. Mascall recently did in his book *The Secularization of Christianity*, aimed mainly at Drs. Robinson, Van Buren, and company. Mascall's attempt is understandable enough, but probably overkill. What I would like to do is probably nastier, and it may not come off, but at least it's worth trying, in self-defense, if nothing else.

Later on in this chapter on the Church and the university, Cox describes three functions that the Church should be undertaking, that require "stepping out of the organizational shells in which they are imprisoned on the hinterlands of the campus [and even more so I would gather, stepping out of so-called Christian colleges and universities, the worst anachronism of all] and [stepping] into the university community itself" (Cox, 226). The three functions Cox elaborates are: (1) restrained reconciliation; (2) candid criticism; (3) creative disaffiliation. I would like to suggest that there is great and even greater validity in pursuing these three churchly functions within the Christian college and university, indeed, that these three functions need doing first and foremost, if the total college and university community in America is to be spared much of what Cox forecasts. I would gladly admit that our Christian colleges and universities need desperately to find themselves, their identity, their special function and high purpose in the totality of American higher education. Maybe Cox has inadvertently helped us in this most important endeavor.

Obviously, I do not intend to apply these three functions in the same context that he does, in the secular university community, since my point is quite apart from his, namely, having accepted the importance of these three functions, they do have a true home and even greater validity within the context of the Christian college and university, especially as these institutions validate their own proper existence and influence the total collegiate and university community in modern-day America. In other words, I grant his substance, but apply his functions quite differently, still, I trust, with no less but even greater ultimate and total effect.

1. Reconciliation

Cox's biblical text for this function is good, although there are many other texts which would illuminate and complement it: "God was in Christ reconciling the world to Himself. And we are ministers of reconciliation." Cox adds: "The Church has no purpose other than to make known to the world what God has done and is doing in history to break down the hostilities between men and to reconcile men to each other" (Cox, 227). Again good, but not far enough. We reconcile men to each other *in Christ and in his love*. The history of salvation is what the Church is about, and this has reference not only between men, but, even more importantly, between men and God. Reconciliation is not the only term for this priestly responsibility. It is even more essentially a work of mediation, for the priest is essentially a mediator, a *pontifex*, a bridge builder. The mediation of God's message to every age must somehow go on, and it is precisely to do this work of mediation that Christian colleges and universities were founded and exist today. They not only transmit to every age the totality of human knowledge in the humanities, in the social and physical sciences, in the professions, but they do this in the context of the Christian saving message. They also do it in the context of the Christian community, in which Christian love is the moving force of reconciliation, and they bolster their efforts by research and vital teaching so that mediation may be continually more effective as knowledge widens. They mediate also by community prayer wherein we admit how little we have really understood the Christian message, yet how very much we do wish to obtain the grace of greater understanding and ultimate wisdom, and, finally, they mediate in Christian service where all our misunderstandings are caught up and redeemed by the Christian giving of ourselves and all we have to others in Christ.

Let it be admitted that we do all of this all too poorly, too unimaginatively, and too ungenerously, but at least our attempts are honest, and perhaps that alone justifies the calling of our colleges and universities Christian. If I might be medieval for a moment, the notion of analogy was then and is now a valid description of the use of words. I do not take the notion of Christian college or university as equivocal, in Cox's terms, but analogical, in the simple sense that what the Bible implies of a person by calling him Christian, that too applies to our institutions, albeit imperfectly, as followers of Christ. It is the spirit that is important here, the intent, the dedication, the commitment. Our institutions, if we try to mediate the saving work of Christ in all we do, are no less Christian than Christian art, or Christian music, or Christian culture. To speak of Christian observatories or laboratories is Cox's point, not ours. We grant his point, but add that it only obfuscates this very real issue of Christian colleges and universities.

The mediator stands in the middle, but he stands for something, else he is a mighty poor mediator. Our Christian institutions are mediators between the believing and the unbe-lieving, the devout and the tepid, the dedicated and the uncom-mitted, the knowing (in the Christian sense) and the ignorant, between those who think the Christian context is important and those who think it negligible. At least we stand for a point of view, in history, in philosophy, in theology, in literature, in art, in music, in drama, in the use of science and technology, in the nature and destiny of man. We know that God has spoken to man and we think this important enough to be reckoned with in all else we know, or believe we know, from whatever source. And we are not about to abdicate the field, whatever Cox says about "the end of the epoch of the Church's dominance in Western culture."

We know that our culture would be poorer today without all that the Church, or better, Christ and his message of salva-tion and faith and hope and charity have brought to it. We are not interested in dominance. We are ready to mediate Christ's message to all forms of human knowledge in institutions sym-pathetic to the message, our Christian colleges and universities, and outside them, too, within the broader collegiate and uni-versity context. Ours is not the concept of a ghetto, but a leaven and a light in the darkness. These images are also biblical. And we apologize to no audience for the weakness of our efforts in view of the greatness of that which we presume to mediate. We are unfaithful servants if we do not try, ever to mediate better, despite the difficulty of the age. Whoever is against us, we might at least assume that Christ and the history of salvation are with us. Thus we proudly, and humbly, bear the name of Christian, ourselves and our institutions.

2. Creative Criticism

Under this rubric, Cox calls for criticism of both the university and the Church. In regard to the university, he is against any world view as being divisive. Here I am reminded of the divisive-ness of Christ: you are either with Me or against Me. Again I am reminded of the testimony of two professors, former Danforth Fellows, at a Catholic and a Presbyterian college:

> Although it may sound paradoxical, I, as a faculty member, feel freer in the Church-related institutions (all Roman Catholic) with which I am familiar. It is a freedom to be myself—to explore and to communicate whatever religious dimensions I, as a religiously-oriented person, find or fail to find within my discipline. I did not feel this same freedom when I taught at non-Church-related institutions, committed, as the faculty and student bodies seemed to be, to a secular materialistic humanism. I found myself squashing areas of investigation and perceptions of religious significance in literature which would have been either totally misunderstood or ridiculed in the secular environment. In the Church-related college, religious meanings and interpretations are understood and encouraged without—and obviously this is essential—forcing them where they do not fit. So, to oversimplify it, *both* the religious and the secular are admitted to the Church-related institution, while *only* the secular are admitted in the secular institution. The result I find to be a greater sense of exploration, a freer intellectual atmosphere, and a greater opportunity to find truth. And from the vantage point of a Church-related college, I feel freer to criticize the failings of my Church. (Patillo-Mackenzie, *Church Sponsored Higher Education*, 168)

The second professor was in the process of moving from a Presbyterian college to a larger state university. He writes, "Let me close by noting an additional satisfaction of teaching in the Christian college which I think may be inherent in that type of institution and hard to find in other types of colleges. It is easy to find other scholars who are interested in the question of how their disciplines and professions relate to the Christian way of life and the Christian faith. One can talk directly and overtly about these questions, rather than obliquely as I anticipate doing at a state university" (Patillo-Mackenzie, 169).

In citing these two professors, I am not attempting to demonstrate that all is rosy and Christlike at our institutions. Even less, am I trying to resuscitate the old antagonism between Christian and state institutions in which the latter are characterized as "Godless." When over 40 percent of state universities today are sponsoring some type of course in religion, it seems to me that with the advantage of the general acceptance of the Christian philosophy of life, in the broadest, most liberal, most ecumenical and open sense of that phrase, in most of our Christian institutions, our most creative criticism of the contemporary scene in higher education would be to demonstrate the meaningfulness of whatever integration and unity of knowledge we have been able to achieve in mediation, in the hope that it will be contagious, not divisive.

In regard to criticism of our Churches, again I do not know where this can be done in a more understanding and creative sense than on our campuses. Here, as nowhere else, the Church meets the contemporary world. I fully agree with the recommendations of the Patillo-Mackenzie report on Church-sponsored education when it says:

> In our judgment, the faculties of Church-related colleges are in the most favorable position to provide intellectual leadership in the study of the issues facing the Church and the hammering out of proposals for action. The Church college lives in both the "Church world" and the "outside world." Its faculty, in the aggregate, has the breadth of knowledge required to see the Church in perspective. College faculties include historians, philosophers, artists, theologians, psychologists, sociologists, literary critics, political scientists, economists—scholars whose business it is to be sensitive to ideas and to understand the meaning of the world around us. They are in touch with

> secular thought, but at their best they care about the
> Church and its future. (Patillo-Mackenzie, 203)

Needless to say, the Church will not receive this kind of creative criticism from the faculty and students of its colleges and universities unless it allows them a maximum freedom to be creative and critical. The Church has nothing to fear from criticism springing from those who love the Church, who want to participate as fully as possible in the continual reformation by which the Church faces each new age and each new problem, by which the Church continually renews herself and purges herself of her many earthly imperfections which are a denial of her total dedication to Christ Our Lord and his saving message. I strongly believe that in default of strong, intelligent, dedicated, and creative criticism within the Church, and especially from within the Church's institutions of higher learning, the Church will suffer the worst kind of carping, sniping, vindictive, and, to say the worst, unloving criticism from those who have already written off the Church, whose unspoken motto seems to be, *ecrasez l'infame*—wipe out the infamy. In a word, if the prophetic, creatively critical mission of the Church-related institution of higher learning is not vital and courageous, the priestly, mediatorial mission will be diminished, even more, in a true and valid sense, suspect. There then would be no easier option for the generality of mankind but to write off the Christian college and university as Cox has done.

3. Creative Disaffiliation

This third function suggested by Cox is the most difficult to apply to our context, instead of his, but it is possible and fruitful, too. First, Cox describes creative disaffiliation as "the modern equivalent of asceticism, the focusing of energy on what is important at the cost of denying what is less important" (Cox, 230). No problem here.

Consistent with his earlier stance, Cox sees the Churches as hindered in their work by "ingrown isolation made unavoidable by the sheer size and complexity of the apparatus and by an institutional and social conservatism related to their dependence on sources of funds, a dependence which in turn precludes the possibility of any real criticism of the structural elements in our society" (Cox, 231).

His advice then is to disaffiliate from this bureaucratic monstrosity. "The university Christian who succumbs to the temptation of work within the organizational Church stands in deadly danger of cutting himself off from the reconciliatory action of God in the world and blinding himself to his place in the drama through which action is taking place" (Cox, 235). As to the Church itself, he asks in the concluding paragraph of this chapter, "What is the role of the Church in the university? The 'organizational Church' has no role. It should stay out" (Cox, 236).

As I said above, it is difficult to apply Cox's third function of "Creative Disaffiliation" to our context, since he has earlier eliminated our context. He is speaking here of the Church and the Christian in the secular university. What I say here depends largely on what I have already said, following his lead in a secular context, on the priestly and prophetic functions of the Christian college and university. One more point must be made here. However one speaks of the Church, as a visible or invisible body, or as both, the Christian college and university are not the Church. And they are very much in the world. We should indeed disaffiliate ourselves from any influence that is not ecumenical, that cuts us off from each other or from the world, or from the very real values that are to be derived from a wider understanding of all the social revolutions in progress.

No age has seen a greater dedication to human dignity, human equality, and human development than our own. No age has had greater resources, educational, scientific, technical and human, to do something about these deepest of human aspirations. Our Christian colleges and universities might well disaffiliate ourselves from our more bland and imitative educational endeavors to throw the full weight of our Christian intelligence and educational dedication into these secular revolutions which may indeed be close to the heart of the mystery of salvation in our times. We have no need to disaffiliate from the Church or from our Christian institutions to do this—but we must respect the validity of new knowledge and new techniques and, relatively, new aspirations. We must understand them on their own terms.

All truth is a part of God's redemptive activity, but all grace is too. And grace, for us at least, comes from another source. Ultimately, both all truth and all grace are from God. More immediately, we seek, find, and respect secular truth in all our institutions of higher learning. We, in Christian institutions, also seek an ever greater understanding of the meaning and relevance of God's divine Word from his revelation. We seek as well God's divine grace, from our deepest fellowship with each other and with him in private and community prayer and in the sacraments. We seek this grace particularly in our Christian institutions of higher learning to inspire, to refresh, and to revivify all our efforts to find and understand all his saving truth in the modern context.

No single facet of this total reality of truth and grace need be denied, nor should any or all of it be confused or underestimated or eliminated, even in an essay, however novel and insightful, as *The Secular City*. There are indeed changing social structures and new functional arrangements following upon the spread of secularization in the world at large and in the world of the intellect. But the lineaments of Jesus Christ and his saving message of grace and truth are yesterday, today, and tomorrow, ever the same.

There may well be new and effective methods of witness in our age. We need not deny them, but in affirming them there is even less need to destroy what in its own unique way may ultimately be more effective, as I believe Christian higher education to be. As the old saw goes, "Don't throw out the baby with the bath water."

If Harvey Cox has spurred us to take a deeper look at ourselves, as Christians, and at our institutions of higher learning, as professedly Christian, if he has piqued us enough to make us redouble our efforts to do more pointedly, more energetically, and with greater focus, the important work we are concerned with in all of our waking hours, then I think we should be grateful to him, even if this was not one of the purposes he had in mind.

At the heart of our specific endeavor are two great educational qualities: commitment and freedom. Have no fear of commitment as long as it is intelligent and deeply believes in real evidence of the truth of those great Christian values to which we are committed. Have no fear of freedom either. It is the context within which commitment grows, deepens, and is enriched, as we freely seek a greater dimension of understanding, a broader unity within the total reality we know, and, hopefully, a better expression of all these values that will speak to the heart of modern humanity in words that they, too, will understand and appreciate. There are all kinds of commitments in the world of higher learning today, scientific, secular, humanistic, agnostic, and all the rest. No one makes any apology for them. We must not be less free than any of them, or less committed. We must even grant them more freedom than they grant us, believing that ultimately the truth makes all of us most free.

I began by speaking of a future challenge. I close with the concluding words of the best study of our Christian institutions, just recently published: "Enough colleges and universities have achieved this combination of commitment and freedom to show beyond doubt that it can be done. We believe that this is the key to the future of Church-related higher education in the United States—the way in which the great tradition of liberal education infused with the Christian faith can, at this point in history, better serve God and man" (Patillo-Mackenzie, 214).

Homily Delivered at Catholic University of Leuven
February 2, 1978

The theme of the day, as all of you have perceived from the liturgical texts, is *light*. We recall especially in the Gospel, the marvelous canticle of the faithful Simeon: "Lord, You now let Your servant go in peace; Your word has been fulfilled; my own eyes have seen the salvation which You have prepared in the sight of every people; a light to reveal You to the nations and the glory of Your people, Israel."

Who can give a better explanation of the raison d'être of the Catholic university than to be a light to reveal Jesus Christ, the Lord and Savior of all the world, to the nations? We also read today in the first lesson from Isaias: "I will make you the light of the nations, so that My salvation may reach to the ends of the earth." What better prophetic calling forth of the exalted mission of the Catholic university?

I need not emphasize to this congregation that we live today in a world of darkness: the ultimate darkness of ignorance and illiteracy that afflicts a fourth of humanity; the inner darkness of life without faith that afflicts other millions; the darkness that is born of pride and its offspring, intellectual blindness; the darkness of sin and greed and cupidity; the darkness of sloth and anomie and of indifference to both the good and the true, not to mention the beautiful. My friends, there is no end to the darkness that surrounds and almost engulfs us all. It is all pervading, enticingly packaged, and depressingly present. Few, if any, of us are strangers to darkness.

We tend at times to think that our age is the worst ever, but I would rather believe that perhaps in this we are unduly pessimistic because we read and see and hear more of the messages of darkness today. . . . We need not propose a superabundance of darkness in the world today, but there is certainly enough darkness to justify the strong and vital presence of this superb

Catholic university. The world still needs an institution that is a light to reveal Our Lord and Savior to the nations.

. . . There was, of course, a day when the light of a university was mainly theological and philosophical. No more. Human knowledge has grown so widely, especially in the natural, biological, and social sciences and in technology, that the present spectrum of light from the modern university must be correspondingly broad. Unfortunately, the expansion of knowledge is, in our imperfect world, also an occasion for the expansion of error. The power of knowledge can be used for evil, as well as for good purposes. To cope effectively with error and this evil, monumental in our times, the university is the only potent intellectual instrumentality in the Church, for both the error and the evil must be deeply understood if they are to be exposed and corrected. The light of the Catholic university in our times must be cast as broadly as the expansive empire of darkness, and with no less intelligence than that which espouses error and promotes evil. We of the Catholic university world must undertake this mission with confidence, for as John reminds us in the beginning of his Gospel of Light: "The Word was God . . . through Him all things came to be, not one thing had its being but through Him. All that came to be had life in Him and that life was the light of men, a light that shines in the dark, a light that darkness could not overpower."

Remarks at the Center for Pastoral and Social Ministry Dinner
University of Notre Dame, September 27, 1978

I'd like tonight to reminisce a bit with you about where we are and where, maybe, we are going. I'd like to do it on the broadest possible scale because we are inclined today to get locked into little corners.

The Catholic university is in a fairly precarious position, in my judgment, in the world today, and to really sense that, you have to go back to the beginning of the university itself. The Italians and the French argue about what was first—Paris or Bologna—but I vote for Paris, which was established by students in 1205. They hired the professors and they fired them, and their university eventually became the great university it is today.

But when you go from there to the growth of Catholic universities—and of course in those days, they were all Catholic—you have such a long list, including Oxford and Cambridge; Louvain in Belgium; Bologna in Italy, and others in Spain and Portugal. But it is interesting to note that the first university world was a Catholic one. The first universities catered to the professions. They had law, they had theology, and they had medicine. And in time, they had the liberal arts and, of course, philosophy. And then a lot of things happened—over a long period of time. The world which the Church had created in the high Middle Ages began to crumble, and with it crumbled the Catholic universities. If you jump from the high Middle Ages, when all higher learning was Catholic, to today, you find that the Catholic university has almost died out in the world, except in this country. . . .

Now, I don't honestly believe that there are going to be a lot of great Catholic universities in America. I wish there were, but I think if we had five or six or ten, I would cheer them. We probably have five that could develop into great Catholic universities, all things being equal. But it will cost an enormous amount of money, and I can only say to you that every day we open the doors here it costs well over a quarter of a million dollars. At those prices we can go broke very quickly. Just having a computer, something that did not exist twenty-five years ago, costs $80,000 a month, and you couldn't possibly run a modern university without it. The budget of the library is about $1.6 million a year, and that's about a half million less than it should be.

I could go on and on, but I think it's obvious to you that we are living in a day when we are faced with an enormous opportunity—an opportunity to create something that has not really existed since the days of the University of Paris and those universities that followed its birth. I think today in this place, and all of you are part of this place, we have a chance to create a great Catholic university. And what is that? How would you differentiate this university called Catholic from the 3,300 universities that exist in this land today?

I think one thing, more than anything else, will characterize this kind of university, as compared to Harvard or Yale or Stanford or Chicago or Penn State. It is something we take almost for granted. We do what all universities do. We search for truth, and we try to transmit the heritage of truth as we know it in our culture and other cultures. We do all manner of research on modern-day problems. We do some amount of service to the society, which is a new part of universities. But I think we begin all this with the belief that God has entered history, which most universities would not admit if backed against the wall with a shotgun. We admit that God has not only entered history, but also has spoken to us. And that his Son, born of Mary, has entered history, and he, too, has given us the Good News. And that somehow life cannot go on as if that didn't happen, historically, and that it has made an enormous difference in how we do anything human from then on, including how a university conducts its business.

It seems to me that, while we do what all universities do, in teaching and learning and researching and serving, we do this in an atmosphere of faith, and we do it with a recognition of God's providence and his grace. This is something over and above the natural phenomena that surround us. And it would seem to me that to be here tonight and to say as each of you may say, "I am part of this," means you are part of something that is growing and evolving, that can be enormously important to a world which is full of moral ambiguity, full of great universities where the majority of the faculty would laugh at what we think most sacred, bound up as they are in scientism and relativism and subjectivism and agnosticism and atheism. And yet when they look at us as a university that does its work in an atmosphere of faith and a search for value and a belief in grace, they think that we can't possibly be a university because we're committed to these things. We are committed to our faith, we are committed to our belief, and those beliefs enter into everything we do, including our research and our teaching and our learning. I would say to them, as I say to you tonight, that I respect them for the commitments they have, and they all have them. They may be commitments to agnosticism. They may be commitments to atheism. They may be commitments to Marxism. I don't care what. There are a whole range of them, fairly held and sincerely offered, and I accept that. I only say that if they can be universities with those kinds of freely accepted commitments, then they should accept this university with our commitments of faith and belief in God's grace and his redemption.

But that leads us to something else. As you know, universities in this country, beginning with the early ones that were called colleges, like Harvard College and Dartmouth College, were founded on the kind of Oxford-Cambridge model of a college. It was Newman's model as well—the British college where people came and learned, and the faculty taught. Subsequently, the influence of the great German research universities created a new role, if you will, for universities, one seen in the foundation of Johns Hopkins as a research university. Beyond teaching came the idea of research, the idea of somehow expanding the frontiers of knowledge within the university itself, enriching those things that are taught.

It wasn't really until the end of World War II when somehow America became the savior of a battered world, that the universities began to take up a third role called service. With service came a wide variety of promises on how we were going to redeem the world. I think we promised too much. I think we faculty, administrators, and others dissipated our energies redeeming these promises, and I think much of the student revolution was due to the fact that we were so concerned with solving the problems of the world that we didn't notice the problems right under our noses.

Today you will find that most universities, most great universities, have pulled back on overextensions of service. The university no longer claims to be able to solve every problem of the world, as well as those in outer space. The universities today have, by and large, stopped having hundreds of their faculty absent. (There was a time when four universities here in the Midwest—Michigan State, Illinois, Indiana, and Wisconsin—had 380 of their faculty overseas at one time. That isn't happening anymore.) Today I think service that goes out of the university is a kind of integral service that is something very special. These are the kinds of services that this university gives in the local community. They are valid and very important. We cannot live here as though in a vacuum. We must relate to the local social needs.

But it struck me, while going over much of this historical data and thinking about the creation of a modern Catholic university, that somehow we're different than a Harvard or a Yale or a Princeton or a Stanford or Chicago. Somehow we do some of the things they do: we have a center for law and the handicapped; we have opportunities for small businesses; we do some overseas work on occasion. But it struck me that if we are going to be a great Catholic university, in the full sense of that word, the most essential service that we should give would be service to the Church.

A university is a place in which many things can happen because of the strengths that exist there—be they theological or philosophical or simply the strength of Catholic community life. We can create things that can't be fashioned in other places.

I have a great hope that, when one writes the history of the university in this period, there will be fine pages in there about our academic growth, the quality of professors who joined us, about research units here and there, and all of the various humanities, sciences, and professions in which we are engaged. But I would think at the same time there would be a few paragraphs, maybe even a few chapters, about how, for possibly the first time in the history of Catholic universities, one university began to see itself in a very special way, in service of the Church that gave it birth, and in which we find our subsistence and our grace. We are in service to a Church beset with many problems that it cannot solve itself, because it doesn't have the intellectual resources, or the libraries, or the caliber of people who can give full time to solving these problems.

But these movements, if you will, or these strands that coalesce in the life of a great university, are not just one-way. It isn't only that we are helping you, or it isn't only that you are helping us. I think we are mutually supportive; we are symbiotic. A university can become a kind of ivory tower, and we have to see how important it is to do our thinking, not in a vacuum or on a mountain top, but in an atmosphere of reality. I have felt that many of the organizations, whether it be CCUM or the retreat movement or pastoral ministry, in many ways refresh or renew us. That they bring into the ivory tower a little of the reality we all need. A kitchen is not really a kitchen unless it is a little cluttered up, and it is important for us, who live here in a rather orderly place, to know that, to cope with it, and to somehow make it a dimension of our thinking.

So what I say to all of you is that you are part of a great adventure. You are part of an adventure that began a long time ago, actually in 1205, if you want to agree with the French and not the Italians. You are part of an adventure that is ongoing at this moment, at this hour. You are part of a Catholic university that strives for greatness. I wish that you would somehow feel that you are part of this great, ongoing endeavor. That somehow you are adding to the reality of the contemporary catholic university, that somehow, in the highest order of academic endeavor which is the university's, you also sense a concern for the moral overlay of human life which makes for human happiness.

This will be a much greater Catholic university if you do your job well, and I am sure you will.

===

Invocation at Inauguration of Dr. William Hickey as President of St. Mary's College
September 7, 1986

What do we pray for him? Again, only a few special blessings: that he be wise for wisdom is what all educational institutions aspire to achieve in its graduates, not just knowledge, but wisdom which transcends knowledge and then courage. No educational institution is easy to lead for there are the great crises, the easy way to go, and then the right way, often the difficult way, the way demanding courage. May he be courageous though there are many other easier solutions and no kudos for being courageous when it means to run against the pack seeking easy and uncourageous solutions. What more do we pray for? That he preserves his sense of humor, because a hundred years from now the great crises will seem ludicrous. May they seem ludicrous today. Also, may he have great faith in you, your Mother, the tradition that has inspired this college for so many years, the faith that none of us is so important as the overarching providence, the bounty of Our Lady, that has kept this place growing, maturing, and persevering for so many years. Dear Lord, our new president is a key actor in all of this for some years to come. . . .

PART VI

LIVES OF ACTION

But if you want the promises of Christ and if you
want the kingdom of heaven, and if you want all
those wonderful things that will happen if you
follow the beatitudes, well, then I think you've
got to take the other side of the loaf, too. We have
to take the kinds of responsibilities and the kinds
of vision of the mind of Christ and the heart of
Christ as it comes to us in the Gospels.

—*Fr. Ted Hesburgh, CSC*

Saved and ever more sanctified by Christ's sacrifice, the faithful
have an indelible call to participate actively in ongoing redemptive work in the world—in the words of the prophet Micah, to
"seek justice, love mercy, and walk humbly with God." Whether
it is tangible care for the poor or championship of civil rights—
indeed, whatever their profession or walk of life—believers
should be compassionately concerned for the suffering and
salvation of humanity, their neighbors. Honoring the inherent
dignity of every human life commits believers to take action for
peace and justice, to resolve conflict and to uplift the needs and
voices of those ignored or silenced. As recipients of and participants in holy work, believers are truly set apart, not relieved of
action but rather empowered to manifest the mind and heart of
Christ throughout a hurting world.

Passionate about civil rights and racial equality, Fr. Ted spoke
often (as in his "Address to the Catholic Interracial Counsel

Communion Breakfast") about how the love of God should and does demand love of neighbor—a love that takes action against suffering and injustice. Many an invocation by Fr. Ted sought those virtues essential to this work—reverence, passion, compassion, dedication, and courage—universally important and perhaps especially so for those in the legal field, uniquely positioned to foster justice. As with justice, Fr. Ted's faith bears a commitment to peace equally on foreign shores ("Untitled Sermon to Notre Dame Family") as in the American courts ("Sermon Delivered at the 'Respect Life' Mass"). In his words, "we, too, would be rather cheap if we couldn't do for others along the lines of what God does for us, so magnificently to give us Himself in so many different ways."

Red Mass Sermon (Catholic Lawyers Guild of Chicago)
November 1, 1953

I live, now not I, but Christ liveth in me.
—Gal 2:20

These brief words of St. Paul are the key to sanctity. Whether a man be a beggar, like St. Benedict Labre, or a bishop, like St. Augustine, his holiness results from Christ living within him by grace. Because of this fundamental truth, the life of every saint is a kind of continuing Incarnation of Christ, so that Christ is permitted to live again on earth and to manifest his saving virtue in every walk of life. Thus, the charity of Christ, the justice of Christ, the very humanity and redemptive kindliness of Christ is made known again to people of every age and every profession in the person of those saints who permit Christ to live in them, and with them, and through them.

Address to the Catholic Interracial Council Communion Breakfast
Chicago, October 25, 1959

I would like to talk today about things that are close to my heart and relating to the general problems of Catholics and civil rights. I think it's a wonderful day to do this, because one of the most modern feast days we have in the whole liturgical calendar is the feast day of Christ the King. I think for each one of us, as persons and as individuals, the feast of Christ the King brings this simple message or, perhaps, this simple question: To what extent does Christ reign in our own hearts and minds? To what extent do we have the heart of Christ? To what extent do we represent in this day and age the instrumentality of our Savior and Redeemer?

You know, it's an amazing thing that Christ being God could have accomplished redemption for all men of all times, as he did, in a very personal immediate way. Yet somehow he wanted to stretch it out across the ages and to use each of us, poor instruments though we may be, priests and laity, to be the instrumentality of bringing him and his wonderful saving presence, his virtue, his whole life, mentality, and spirit to a world that is somewhat lost and disorganized without it.

For each of us this whole question of civil rights and our participation in the city of men is not just a social thing, or an emotional thing, or an exigency of the moment. It is first and foremost and fundamentally a theological problem, a moral problem, a spiritual problem. And it can only be settled, ultimately, in terms of what our basic beliefs are, as Christians and as Catholics.

I have often wondered at the dichotomy between the Catholic faith, which is pretty clear-cut on this, and Catholic practice, which is somewhat muddled at times, if you have to judge it from the lives of individual Catholics, here or in any other country of the world.

I suppose this is why we have feasts like Christ the King so that somehow each Catholic may be confronted with this question: To what extent does Christ reign in my life? To what extent do I have the mind of Christ? To what extent do I speak the thoughts of Christ and think those thoughts deeply and believe them? To what extent does my heart and its emotions represent the emotions of Christ, if you will, his compassion, his love, his justice, his generosity, his interest in every human being who ever lived or whoever will live?

You know, there was a first Communion breakfast of all times and, strangely enough, it is called the Last Supper. But this first Communion breakfast was an occasion for remarks much more profound than anything I will have to say this morning. And if I would take a general theme for my remarks, it would be from Our Lord's words at that Last Supper, where he said, "By this shall men know that you are My disciples: That you love one another as I have loved you."

If we want a measure for the extent of our love for other persons, for other human beings, we have the magnificent measure of God's love for us, of Christ, Our Lord's love for us. And to try to put some dimensions on that almost impossible love of God for man, his infinite wisdom and generosity. I like to think of a sermon I got once by a French Dominican called Lasaubret. In this sermon, he talks about what he calls the "divine communications." And he says, as he gave the sermons at the Cathedral of Notre Dame in Paris during the Lenten season, "What has God really given to man?" He starts out in the natural order: God has given us a mind and a will, and in this we are indeed Godlike, made to God's image and likeness, because of all creation we are the only members of creation that can think, the only members that can really choose and love. And in this, these two functions, we become persons, as God himself is personal.

Then, not satisfied with this, he says, our God takes upon himself human nature. He becomes a man with all the weakness of man. He was hungry as man was hungry. He needed sleep. He felt the need for companionship. He wept at the death of his friends. And he took all of our human frailty, even the power of suffering that a God-man could suffer in all its infinity and he offered this up for our salvation.

Still he was not satisfied with this, because this suffering was for some purpose, namely, our redemption. He accomplishes this redemption through our rebirth in Christ in Baptism, where he comes himself to dwell in our souls and each of us who is baptized may surely say that we are temples of God, that we partake in the Divine Nature, that somehow, through Grace, God dwells in us.

Not satisfied with this great gift of his own self, which makes us Christians, our rebirth in Christ, all along the way with our fumblings and our stumblings, he nourished us with his own Body and Blood, and it was this indeed, this act of nourishment,

that brought you together primarily for a Communion breakfast. And he offers himself, not only once at Calvary, but daily
in every church in the world and on the altar of the Mass, to
renew this Sacrifice and to apply it to our day and our age, and
to give each of us the impression of Christ anew in our souls and
his presence within us so that we can go forth and try to act in
a Christlike fashion, to try to think like Christ, to try to feel, if
you will, like Christ.

And not satisfied with all this, because all this is looking
toward the consummation of the great gift of God to us, ultimately he gives us a vision and a complete possession of himself
in what is called, theologically, the Beatific Vision. But not just a
vision of all that is good and beautiful and an understanding of
all that is in this world and of our universe, but a full embracing
love of all of this and a possession never-ending of all of this
and, in this, to possess all the good things that we've sought
through life, and to somehow gather together into this Beatific
Vision the totality of our wildest hopes, if you will, and of our
best strivings and to have this forever, and in this to be indeed
supremely happy with God.

Well, now I ask you, if this is the measure of our love for
our fellow men—what God has done for us—and if this is what
he has done for us, then try to think for a moment what we are
asked to do to our fellow men on this pattern. You all recall the
time the scribe came up to Our Lord and he said, "What's the
main commandment?" And Our Lord said, "Well, what do you
think?" And he said, "Thou shalt love the Lord, thy God, with
thy whole heart and with thy whole soul and thy whole mind and
thy neighbor as thyself." And Our Lord said, "You have spoken
rightly." But then the man said, "But who is my neighbor?" And
then came forth the wonderful story of the Good Samaritan.

Now we all know the story. But I think the interesting thing
is that when Our Lord told that little parable, to illustrate who is
our neighbor, he picked a man in trouble, a man who had been
set upon, who lay wounded by the side of the road. And he spoke

of the high and mighty who walked by, including a Pharisee and a priest. Now the Samaritan, who was indeed supposed to be an outcast, bound up the man's wounds and took him to an inn, paid for his keep, and said: "If there is any more, I will stop and pay the rest of the bill when I return."

But who is our neighbor today, in this day and age? Again I think, our neighbor, in the most poignant fashion and in the most telling fashion, is the person in difficulty. And this brings me to one more attempt to get somewhere near the mind of Christ on this whole matter of love and justice—the mind of Christ that we must exemplify if Christ is King in our hearts and in our minds. That is the wonderful example that Our Lord gives of the Last Judgment, of the judgment that all of us some day must face of how we have used the talents that God gave us and how we have spent our lives. The interesting thing is Our Lord knew the commandments full well, and he knew the things that are on people's minds when they think of being moral or immoral, things like sex, stealing, and all of the other so-called horrible sins. And yet when it came to exemplifying what God was going to say on the Last Day, Our Lord didn't pull out what might be called these dramatic sins. He said on the Last Day he was going to say to one group of people, "Come, ye blessed of My Father, into the kingdom which is prepared for you from all eternity." And then to others he is going to say, "Depart, ye cursed, into everlasting fire which was prepared for the devil and his followers." And then he said the people are going to ask, "Well, Lord, why? Why this judgment? Why do some go to heaven and some go to hell?"

Then he gave the illustration of the means by which he was going to judge. And it was so simple you might think that he was really not up on his Commandments and he had missed the big dramatic sins. Because what he said is: "I was hungry and you gave Me something to eat. And I was thirsty and you gave Me something to drink. And I was naked and you clothed Me. And I was in prison and you visited Me." And he said then the people will say, "Well, Lord, when did we see You hungry and thirsty and naked and in prison and do these things for You?" And he said, "Whatever you did for one of these, my least brethren, you did it for Me." And here we come to the real notion of the kingdom of God, that what we do for anyone, the least brethren, the man most in trouble, our neighbor, the one closest to us and in trouble, what we do for this person is the same as a perfect act of the love of God. We do it for God himself, and he is identified in this person.

. . . And it came home to St. John of God, as I just quoted you from Our Lord's own words, "Whatever you do to one of these, my least brethren, you do it to Me."

Now, if you measure up to this dimension of charity, people will know we're Christians or Catholics. They will know that we really follow Christ by the way we love one another, by the way we love our neighbor as ourselves. Our love for God, our love for men, is patterned on God's own love for us and what he has done for us—what he has done for all mankind, spiritually. I think you'll agree with me that the things we're asked to do are pretty small and pretty puny compared to what God has done for us. And I think we, too, would be rather cheap if we couldn't do for others along the lines of what God does for us, so magnificently to give us himself in so many different ways.

I've always found it incomprehensible, and I speak as a priest in this, that so many Catholics can be so wonderful in so many ways, so generous to good causes, so personable in their family life, so faithful to their wives, so loving to their children, so good in many ways, perhaps maternalistic might be a better word in some ways. But, despite this, they are so unconcerned and so wrong about matters of what might be called social morality.

There are so many Catholics I know, good and wonderful people, who in their personal lives and in their individual morality are about as close to 100 percent as one could hope to be—perhaps much more than I am personally. And yet, in their social thought, they are about as anachronistic as a dinosaur. They are completely out of step with the mind of Christ and the mind of the Church, the word of the encyclicals, the letters of the bishops—the basic Catholic doctrine. And I think it's important that those of us who do want to concern ourselves—and apparently you are concerned or you wouldn't be here—do feel at least that there is some deep spiritual, moral reason for being here and for the things we do. That perhaps might help you in talking to your fellow Catholics who may not do as much or may not be interested in doing as much.

When you look at the doctrine of the Church in its most fundamental principles, it is just impossible for a person who really believes and thinks this to be unjust in an interracial way or in any other way, or to be uncharitable in an interracial or any other way.

You look, for example, at the basic doctrine of the unity of the human race—that we all came from two parents, Adam and Eve that, if you go back far enough, all of us have the same human blood, we have the same human nature. You can go deeper than that and say that one Savior came and gave his life for all of us, literally all of us. When you stop to think that in our purpose in living as Christians, we are aiming at the same goal to be shared together and somehow we must help each other along the way. If you look at the very word *Catholic*, which means universal and comprising all, excluding none, and if you take the total complexion of what this means, to have one God, one heaven, one Creator, one Redeemer, and one common human nature, then on top of that to say we cannot offer equal opportunity to all, that we must discriminate between this type and that type, or this race or that race—the thing is simply so incomprehensible that one stops to wonder if somehow the message didn't get through or the message wasn't heard.

Maybe we priests are at fault that we don't preach this doctrine often enough. Or perhaps our laity is at fault in not plummeting deeply enough in the faith that is theirs and the reasons for that faith.

. . . Well, the point behind all of this is that we must be terribly concerned about the deep problems that beset the City of Man in our day and age. As Catholics we can't possibly extricate ourselves from these problems, except at the cost of being less Catholic than we should be. Somehow we must through conversation, through persuasion, through what we do in our own lives most of all, bring home to all Catholics that the kingdom of God is not something that came ready-made upon earth. It is something that must be made each day. Indeed, it must be made in each one of our lives, and it is an up-and-down process, as you and I know. To have the mind of Christ means to think of all things as Christ would think of them. To have the heart of Christ is to have the kind of compassion and human understanding for all human problems that Christ himself would have.

And I think some Catholics—unless this word gets through somehow to them and unless they can plead crass ignorance of the subject matter and of the demands of their Catholic life—some of them are going to be in for a terrible surprise. Some of them, when they get to the pearly gates someday may ask in the greatest surprise, "Well, why is this happening to me?"

I think Our Lord is going to say, "I was hungry and you didn't give Me anything to eat, and I was thirsty and you didn't give Me anything to drink, and I was naked and you didn't clothe Me, and I was in prison and you didn't visit Me."

And they are going to say, "Lord, we never saw You during life. How did we not do these things for You?"

He is going to say, "Whenever you refused to do it for one of these, My least brethren, you did it to Me. You refused to help Me."

We have to let our minds run a bit on these standards that I didn't make up this morning. I merely quote from Christ Our Lord, whose kingdom we celebrate today. It is Christ Our Lord who tells us this in a way that should get home to all of us—that there are all kinds of people in America, not just Negroes. There are people of all races and of all creeds in America who are literally hungry for a little recognition, for a little opportunity, for a little respect for what they are as human beings, for a chance to better themselves, for a little affection even.

They literally hunger for this. And each one of us must someday stand before God and answer not just for the personal, individual morality that our lives represent, but for the social morality from which we cannot extricate ourselves unless we want somehow to leave the human race.

We have to admit that there are people in the world who really thirst, who thirst for justice, who are being persecuted, who thirst again for the kind of life that is the legitimate longing of every human being, to make something of one's life, to make some contribution to society, to be loved and respected, and not just to be someone who is kicked around from this little place to that. What do we do to give something to drink to those who thirst in this way, whose lives somehow touch our own lives? I think we can easily think of the people who, in this country today and throughout the world, are naked. Not just naked physically, but naked of the kinds of supports and buttresses that should be around any human being—who is of a spiritual nature and who is going to have an eternal destiny, a human being that God thought enough of that he became a human being in Christ Our Lord at Christmas and that he lived and died for and told how to live and die. He gives us himself, his own Divine Life in Baptism and gives us himself as our food along the way.

What do we do to clothe people who are naked as to their civil rights and as to their merely human longings? People who are naked of any kind of respect or any kind of normal protection of freedom? People who can't even live in a decent place if they want to, because they're just excluded, because of some irrelevant factor, having nothing to do with their worth as human beings? People who can't work at a certain job, because it just isn't done and no one has enough nerve to go against the stream and say, "If you're as good as the next person, you can work here." People who can't even go to this or that school, because it just isn't done?

People who perhaps cannot even deal with their own family, their own children, to give them the kinds of hopes, the kinds of dreams that every parent wants to give his children?

There are people, naked in this way in our country, in our neighborhoods, today, in our city, here in Chicago. As to people in prison, the same analogy holds true. There are people indeed in prison today as to the expansiveness of their human nature, and to the dignity of their human personality, as to the kind of respect they lack for what God has done for them in making them human beings and what he has done in addition in calling them to be Christians.

Now can a person say he's a Christian and, *a priori* a Catholic, and still have attitudes that run completely counter to what I have been saying? The fact that I am saying it doesn't mean very much—I am just another priest out of some forty-five or fifty thousand priests in this country, several hundred thousand perhaps in the world. But I think that my case, as I have given it, is based upon the mind of Christ and on the words of Christ. And I know that my case, as I've given it to you dogmatically, is founded upon the Catholic faith. There is one strange thing about the Catholic religion: No one has to belong to it. But if you want to belong to it, you've got to accept it at face value. You can't pick "a, b, c, d" and leave off "e, f, g." If you take the Catholic faith, you either take all of it or you take none of it. You can't pick and choose because, as it stands, it is founded upon the word of Christ Our Lord. And Our Lord said some things that were very pleasant. And he said some things that were quite unpleasant, like eternal fire. But you can't pick the one and discard the other. No Catholic can. And I'm afraid that perhaps the Catholic Church scandalizes our day and age in some of its own membership—that somehow in their own lives they tend to pick some parts of Catholicism and reject others.

I'm willing to admit that we're all creatures of our families, of our neighborhoods, and the kinds of standards we grew up with. But I think we come face to face on a great feast day, like the feast day of Christ the King, asking ourselves honestly: What is the mind of Christ in this or that great issue?

I can quote the President of the United States as saying that the issue of civil rights is our greatest present domestic issue, upon the resolution of this issue depends, in large measure, the world leadership of the United States in a world that is at least two-thirds colored. If we are going to be consistent in our world leadership, there must be a consistency about what we do at home. And no person can absolve himself from some responsibility in this most pressing of all problems at home. Beyond that, no Catholic worthy of the name can act one way and still claim to be a Catholic. Of course, any Catholic is free to stop being a Catholic when he wants to.

But if you want the promises of Christ and if you want the kingdom of heaven, and if you want all those wonderful things that will happen if you follow the Beatitudes, well, then I think you've got to take the other side of the loaf, too. We have to take the kinds of responsibilities and the kinds of vision of the mind of Christ and the heart of Christ as it comes to us in the Gospels.

I don't think anybody in this room, and least of all myself, wants to say that any one of us perfectly represents the mind of Christ. There are too many patches and tatters on all of our lives. But if the mind of Christ is clear on one thing, I think it is clear on the fact that we have one God for Our Father and Christ Our Lord for our Brother. That we have one destiny, that we share the same means, that our salvation is not for this or that group, but for all of us, and that we, as Catholics, must be interested in everybody, not just other Catholics, but all people of all races. And that in doing this we must somehow represent the understanding, the compassion, the mind of Christ.

I hope that, having been together at Holy Communion this morning, having received the same Lord into your hearts, having participated in the same sacrifice of Calvary, renewed at the altar, I would hope that underneath all your efforts in this organization and underneath all the so-called companionship that takes place around these tables, somehow inside your life something very real takes place, that isn't seen today and that is not manifest to anybody except yourself—that somehow inside your life you try, no matter what it costs, to have the mind of Christ and to have, not just the willingness to sit at a table with each other, but somehow to respect each other and, indeed, to love Christ in each other, because in this you shall be known as Catholics and Christians and disciples of Christ—that we love one another as he has loved us.

Invocation at the Dinner of the Civil Rights State Advisory Committees
June 27, 1964

Lord God, Father of all our people, grant us, we pray, the special virtues we need in this hour of decision. Grant us, first of all, a deep and heartfelt *reverence* for the innate dignity of every human being made in your image and likeness.

Grant us *compassion* for all who suffer injustice, indignity, and persecution.

Grant us a *passion for justice* that all our people may enjoy equality to live and grow as human dignity requires.

In an age when all too little really care, grant us a *sense of dedication and commitment*, realizing that whatever we do for one of these, your least brethren, we are doing for you, and serving you.

Grant us *courage*, for wisdom without courage is sterile, and nothing will be done in our day without meeting the basic requirement of courage: that we not only believe in human dignity, but are willing to stand up, to work, yes, even to suffer to achieve it.

Armed with reverence for your image in all our brethren, compassion for those who suffer, a burning passion for justice, a sense of dedication and courage to act—grant that we can move forward to achieve in our times the great dream that brought our country into being.

We thank You this day for the great blessings of America, we confess our considerable faults, prejudices, and inequities, and we do pray for your grace today to rededicate ourselves to do your will which is our justice, our love, and our peace.

Invocation at the Inaugural Convocation, Antioch School of Law— Washington
November 13, 1972

. . . If we might ask one special blessing today, it would be for the students—those pioneer beginners, and the long generations of students yet to come here with their hopes. May theirs ever be a hunger for justice. May they ever realize that lawyering without justice is a kind of prostitution. May they seek competence in the law, since compassion without competence would be a cruel hoax upon those they serve. May they also realize that competence in the law without compassion leads the lawyer to use the law for other purposes than the works of justice, blinds him to the sad plight of persons who suffer injustice for want of a lawyer champion. May these students in their lawyer lives ever avoid that which bends the noble law to ignoble ends: to the attaining or the preservation only of power, status, excess income or even injustice sustained by legal manipulation. May these students learn the majesty of the law in this place, and through the practice of law, may they earn for themselves and others the blessings of the God of justice, not the least of which is personal and civic peace, which is at the same time both the noblest work and the finest fruit of justice among just men working for the creation of a just society—a never-ending task.

Finally then, may I invoke upon all of you in the name of God that most ancient blessing which is likewise a greeting, a send-off on a journey, a good wish for you all, Shalom—Peace.

Sermon to Notre Dame Family
Cease Fire in Vietnam, January 28, 1973

I greet fellow priests and all of you members of the Notre Dame family who are here together to offer this holy sacrifice of the Mass with us, and to share what I hope will be a Christian reflection on our times. I suppose the first thing someone might ask coming into the hall today is, "Why are we here?" When one thinks of the Mass, one thinks of a celebration. It has been said so many times in recent days there is really nothing to celebrate today; there is no real victory for anyone; there is no certain peace for anyone. The least that we can grasp and be happy about and thank God for is that for now the guns are silent for the first lasting period in ten years in our history and thirty years in the history of the Vietnamese.

. . . Let us pray for all who suffer and who will carry the physical and moral marks of this war in their bodies and souls for the rest of the days of their lives as spiritual or moral or physical cripples. Let us pray for all the dispossessed, all the imprisoned, all those who have alienated themselves from their times and their country. Let us pray for all those whose lives have been in any way poisoned by this war, including those who have profited from it. And let us pray most fundamentally for healing for our people, our times, and our world.

. . . And anyone who has read any books or watched any television knows of that country which is physically, morally, and spiritually devastated. Filled with the human detritus of war, of graves and orphans and widows, and cripples and illegitimate children and prostitutes and pimps and thieves and ghettos and slums where once there was beautiful countryside and the jade

green of growing rice. I can only recall what a young Vietnamese girl told me once in the airport at Saigon—*C'est triste*—"it's
sad"—and even today, with peace hopefully beginning, the total
picture of that country is sad, and we bear the largest or at least
the equal responsibility of making it as sad as it is.

I am not here today to pass blame or to recriminate, but to
try with you to understand what has happened, not just there,
which is to our shame, but here in our own country. And while
one cannot recall all that has happened in this ten years of time
in the few moments available to me, let can just touch on a few
of the points that come home to roost strongly. I think that never
before since the Civil War has our country been so frustrated, so
divided, so disunited. There has been the cleavage of the young
and the old, the cleavage between those who saw the war as an
obscenity and those of the military industrial establishment and
the government who prosecuted the war, with enthusiasm at
times. There has perhaps never before in our history been such
a cleavage between the military and the civilian, at times for the
wrong reason, but there it was nonetheless.

There has never been a time when the most sensitive people in our society, those morally sensitive to values as to what
is right, have been more alienated to their own country, many
to the point of leaving it. The war also brought a new kind of
unthinking violence to our country, even a threat to the rationality and civility that should characterize universities. And this
whole counter-culture that has developed has somehow brought
on a new fascism which I think is perhaps the worst threat to all
that America stands for: its freedom and dignity and its values.

There has also been that great devaluation of the quality of
American life. I have often spoken of it as anomie, a rootlessness,
a valuelessness. It is best seen in the violence and the killing
that the war symbolizes and reflects throughout our nation. It is
symbolized in the kind of debasement of language where killed
human beings are spoken of as body counts in each evening's
news, so many hundreds, so many thousands, until we simply

couldn't cope with the thought of that many human beings violently killed that day.

. . . We have, I think, as a nation been so shocked into a kind of moral insensitivity so that it is difficult today to get people excited about anything, no matter how evil. I would say, by parenthesis, that we could have never come as far, as quickly as we have, in the whole field of abortion today had it not been the cheapening of sense of the sacredness and the dignity and the value of every human being, no matter how helpless or how incipient.

I think, too, we have seen the moral debasement of many good people who for their moral sensitivity and courage have been put in jail or made to be pariahs in the society of our times. We have driven many young people to drugs, not that one forgives it, but it is sad to see them doing it somehow to forget the nightmare, to create a false world in which one might live with some happiness, apart from the world that was being created with such unhappiness. We have seen people that the society needs, people of courage, people of conviction, people of moral sense driven from any participation in its work because somehow they were disloyal to this mammoth juggernaut that had to ride roughshod over lives and people far away.

. . . It was said of a Mexican poet named Paz, a Spanish word meaning peace, that he could so stand back and look at the world in his poetry, that he could visualize the past without love and yet not look at the future with any panic. I would like to say today that having taken this brief look at the past, I think that you and I and all of us must look to the future without panic; we must certainly look at it with love and I think we should also look at the future with hope and courage and dedication. If we've learned anything in the years that have passed, the sad decade that we are just completing, I would hope that you students should have learned the foolishness of war.

. . . The second lesson I think we have to admit today is that the only victory possible to us, and I would repeat the only victory with honor, is what we do to make this peace that stretches out with great fragility ahead of us. And I do not think that peace is possible in our times unless all of us become more concerned about justice, about the fact that mankind is one wherever he is and in whatever condition, and that the welfare of the world is closely linked to our own welfare as people and as a nation. I think it is difficult to describe peace, but it certainly cannot be described as simply as the absence of people firing guns and cannons at each other or dropping bombs on each other.

I think one must say if one looks at the world today, that peace is not possible, except insofar as we are working for justice. The creation of peace means making hope possible for people who have little enough hope in life, working for human development here and elsewhere throughout the world.

Somehow I think we find it more difficult to see virtue up close than we do from afar. To try to shrink the world for you, I take you to the moon and I ask you to look at that beautiful small globe of blue, white, and green whirling in the darkness of space. And I ask you to think of it as a spaceship with not 3.5 billion people aboard, but with only five people aboard, as one can think of five people while it is difficult to think of 3.5 billion people. And on that spaceship, there are just so many resources, just so many possibilities of hope for health, education, and welfare of all kinds. And on that spaceship, there are limited resources, there is just so much of everything and no more. And what there is cannot be replaced, and what is used or wasted or destroyed or perverted cannot be brought back again.

On that spaceship today one of those passengers—one of the five—represents all of us in the Western world, the world of Europe and America. And that one who represents us has 80 percent of all of the resources of that spaceship at his disposal and the other four persons have to divide up the other 20 percent, having thus 5 percent apiece. That is all they have, and they live in this cramped and shrinking world of a spaceship seeing us with a lion's share—80 percent—and with the four of them only having 20 percent to share among themselves. And their 20 percent is shrinking right now to 10 percent and the other 10 percent is coming to us who already have 80 percent.

I ask you what chance is there for peace or understanding or love or justice aboard such a spaceship? That indeed, my friends, is the picture of the earth today. And if you want to bring it closer to home, of the one person representing 20 percent of mankind, we as a nation represent 6 percent of mankind. And we alone as a nation are using 40 percent of all the world's resources for our own purposes—selfish or not, luxurious or not. And I say to you that that is not justice and that it cannot continue if there is to be justice in this world. I ask you this day if you want peace. What are you willing to sacrifice for peace? Because sacrifice indeed we must if justice is going to come to the rest of the world.

It is easy to speak of peace and justice far away in Vietnam, but think of it at home because that is where it must begin in your heart and mine—think of peace in families, think of peace in neighborhoods and in schools, think of peace between races—blacks and whites, browns and whites—think of peace between ethnics for, in a peaceful world, one ethnic group cannot set itself up against another and ask, "What am I getting?" And if you who are young today and have a chance to remake this world want to be one thing, I say to you to be a mediator to somehow begin to bring the process of bridge building to be a reality among the young and the old, between men and women, between the rich and the poor, between those who never had it so good and those who are suffering injustice, between those who don't have to worry about human dignity and those who are affronted in their human dignity every day of their lives, between those who have hope and those who are without hope.

I would have to say to most of you in this hall today that you are on the best side of every one of these equations because you have hope and you have means and you have education and you have what peace you can take to yourself and you have justice, but the world will have greater peace and justice only to the extent that you are willing to take what you have and pass it along and to work for the achievement of justice and peace in our times. You will be a peacemaker, only to the extent that you bridge the polarities that separate so many people in our society. And only to that extent will you enjoy what St. James mentioned in the Epistle today as the "harvest of peace."

We have some problems still facing us. The main problem I have been speaking about is the problem of uniting and reuniting and healing all in America. The enormous problem of renewing our values, not our values in the macro sense that we are against poverty in the world but will do nothing about giving up something to help those who are poor; not the macro values like condemning justice in the military industrial establishment that is making profit out of the war but not condoning the fellow who is being unjust in a chemistry exam because he happens to be one of us and maybe we are unjust, too. Not just talking about peace far away and then fighting with your roommate—peace and justice have to be micro values—virtues that touch you and your life, as well as virtues that are practiced afar and in the field.

I think the greatest reality I can wish for you is that you be concerned for meaning in your lives, for a life so lived that when you get to be the age of your mother and father you can say, "I tried to make a better world." Not condemning us who are older today, but taking a task upon yourself and trying to have us work with you, as indeed we must to achieve a better world. I think that one also would say that one of the unfinished parts of the business that faces us today is to somehow strain ourselves a little to bring back into the fullness of this society in which we live in America those who have been totally alienated from it, simply because they could not accept its values in the time of war. I think of all those who are in prison today because they stood up and said, "I will not serve in such an immoral conflict." I think of some 70,000, more than the number killed in Vietnam, who went to places like Canada or Sweden and who said, "I can't live in this country if it means I will have to take part in something I don't believe in." I think of those who have suffered all kinds of indignities, all kinds of name-calling because they have played the part of the prophet and told us what we should hear and didn't want to hear. And I think of the great moral value it has been to this country that so many young people have put their lives on the line so to speak, who went to jail or went abroad simply because they wanted to show that they really believe something so deeply that they would put their life on the line for it.

I think the country should cherish people like this—I don't think every case is the same and every case must be evaluated separately—but I think there is so much goodwill and so much virtue in all of this that it deserves a little effort on our part to see that many of these people are brought back into the fullness of our society.

I would like to say in conclusion that there is only one real answer for all of you who have many years of life ahead of you, and that is that as you educate yourself for competence in whatever you want to do in life, you also try to educate yourself in value because that is something you must do for yourself. It can't be done for you. And when you educate yourself for value, ask yourself how much your competence is going to be used just for yourself and how much for this creation of a better world. And ask yourself as you develop competence how much of it are you willing to dedicate to create a world that might live in peace and not in war, that might create hope instead of devastation for human beings who are already badly devastated. Ask yourself how much your generation is willing to give to restore Indo-China to some kind of human hope now that so much money and so many lives have been given to disrupt and destroy it.

I suspect that this will be swimming upstream all the way because, curiously, it is easy to get money for destruction and it's difficult to get money to develop mankind in this world. But this is your challenge and it begins today. I would say that it is easy to criticize the world that our generation has made. It is easy to criticize it as useless and hopeless and, like the poet named Paz, you cannot really look on this world with great love—the world of the past decade. But neither need you look at the world ahead with panic and neither need you look ahead with anything but courage and hope and dedication and love. And if you do that, then indeed we will have something to celebrate here today.

God bless you all.

Sermon Delivered at the "Respect Life" Mass, Sacred Heart Church
January 22, 1975

> I have come that you may have life and have it more abundantly.
> —*words of the Gospel just read*

My dear friends, two years ago today the U.S. Supreme Court made one of its less brilliant decisions. In fact, I think what will over time be seen as one of its most faulty decisions on the very center of what is most important in this world—that which we celebrate this evening—the mystery of life. I do not think that this is an unusual thing—that a group of human beings makes a faulty decision. Although one would hope that on this level of jurisprudential judgment in an area that concerns rights, the judgment might be more solemnly structured and more fittingly argued than it was. And I think all who have studied it from where we sit see it as a very superficial, poorly argued and badly rendered decision.

I say it was not the first time it happened. Toward the close of the last century there was another important decision given by the Supreme Court of the U.S. regarding rights, and it was called *Plessy vs. Ferguson.* And what it said was that if you happened to be black instead of white you were equal but in a separate kind of way. And it was over a half century later that another Supreme Court said that's not right—that separate and equal really has meant and does mean today separate and unequal. Blacks educated in the South are educated separately and unequally. One spends one-fourth the amount of money on them as one spends on white education. And blacks are cut off from every aspect of American life and treated with the highest indignity and all of this in the name of *Plessy vs. Ferguson*. And it went on for over fifty years until the *Brown* decision of 1954, under the leadership of Chief Justice Earl Warren.

There was, of course, dissent to that original decision as there was dissent to the decision of two years ago. And one would hope that one would not have to wait fifty years for the redress of the wrong that has been done. One is watching a nation torn apart because of this. We are brought up to respect the law and it is difficult to respect the law on the one hand while railing at the law's highest court on the other. But if we think we must, we should. But we should do so with civility and with respect and with persuasion.

Tonight we celebrate the mystery of life. That mystery begins in the life of a Godhead. It really doesn't begin at all. It always was and always will be and it exists, that life of God— Father, Son and Spirit—in a most mysterious triune fashion. In fact it is the highest mystery of theology—the Trinity. And we read in the first reading tonight how God created the world, and how the pinnacle of that creation was life. And it was at the pinnacle because it reflected the life of God himself—a life of intelligence and a life of freedom—a life so splendid in its dignity because it was Godlike. And then Our Lord came, like us, born of woman, and he said he had come that we might have life and have it more abundantly than we do now on this earth in this temporal order. And he told us how we would be born again and, indeed, all of us were in the baptism of water and the Holy Spirit. And in that way we shared the life of God himself, so that God himself lives within each one of us this day if we are in grace. And that passing from this life to eternal life will be no great change—but simply a flowering and a vision and the sight of what we have within us at this very moment.

This mystery of life is what really is at the heart of our concern, because we say that it is a gift so stupendous, so magnificent, so mysterious that no one but God has any rights over it. And even God to our knowledge does not abuse the right that he has over life. He gives it abundantly, mysteriously to be true, but abundantly and richly throughout the world in all kinds of varieties—in plants and animals and most of all in man.

There is that mysterious moment when man and woman collaborate to create a body and then they collaborate with God to create a soul. And somehow through the action of man and woman and God there is brought into life a human being. You can argue forever and ever about what this human being is at what stage of his or her development. And there is no reason I know of philosophically or theologically that can say it's *now*, it's *then*, except we know that once life begins, it moves along in an inexorable path to be what it was created to be.

Some of these human beings are not born—some by sheer accident of miscarriage, thousands and perhaps millions each year, and others by the will of man and woman—also millions each year. Over the first, miscarriage, we have no control. We leave the fate of that human being in the eyes of God. In the second case, where it is the result of human action, we feel terribly wounded, as we should. Because somehow someone has arrogated to himself or herself the omnipotent power of God to say this being shall live and this other being shall not live. And that is a lawful act—which we can never believe it is. You might say, if it's all that simple why do so many people think that they are right and we are wrong? And here in a way we have the crux of the great challenge that faces each of us. No law of man can by decree or judgment say that what is wrong in the eyes of God suddenly becomes right. Who knows the depth of depravity that has been said or done in the name of law—the highest law of the land. It was under the highest law of Germany that six million Jews were burned in incinerators, and the people who did that can say, "we were following the will of our fuehrer, Mr. Hitler, and we were following the orders of our legitimate civil authorities," as they were. And yet they were obscenely wrong in the name of the law.

And people today can say now that the Supreme Court has said it is lawful, we can do it, and that it is legitimate. But one can still say on reflection and with deep conviction that it is obscenely wrong. And yet we are faced in our country in our times with a divided nation on this issue. And we have to ask ourselves why this is so and what might be done about it. Curiously, those who are at the very fount of life, those who are the nurturers of life, women, are in the forefront of those proposing the legitimacy of abortion as a very sacred woman's right. It may be difficult for you and for me to understand this. But it is a fact that nine out of ten people you see arguing abortion happen to be women, and they are arguing it in the name of Women's Liberation. I happen to believe in Women's Liberation, but I do not believe in this deduction from Women's Liberation—that abortion is a fundamental right of women. I think women have no more right over the life of an unborn human being than I have or anyone else. And if God does not exercise that right, then neither should we.

Some of the people I have known to be most apostolic in the area of supporting human rights are also most apostolic in promoting the right of abortion, as it is called in their nomenclature. Even some of those who have most suffered from the lack of rights—one of my famous friends who is a black civil rights leader—one of the best in this world. I heard him say on television two or three nights ago, "I'm in favor of abortion."

You might ask yourself, how did it all happen? It seemed for a while that it wasn't going to happen until it happened in New York and it happened in California and then suddenly there was a bit of a surge against it in Michigan and other states and then suddenly out of the blue came the Supreme Court judgment, which I think few people expected but many cheered, many millions cheered. And following that they had, with the respectability of the law, gone about their ways procuring abortions by and large for a variety of reasons but often for simple convenience, which seems a terrible judgment upon the sacredness of human life—that it's convenient or inconvenient and on the basis of inconvenience it might be snuffed out. But this is what we face, and I tell you this evening that if we are not to wait fifty long years to do something about it, we had best be more strategic than we have been to date in doing something about it.

I am not here tonight, and it is not part of a homily, to tell you what the best strategy is as far as definite ways and means of righting what we think is desperately wrong. But I can tell you some things that I think in the name of the respect for life and the cherishing of life that we must pay more attention to as Catholics. First of all, let us say that life is not simply to be respected and to be defended before birth but after birth as well. And that respect for life means respect for all of those things that make life truly human and truly Christian, and the right to decent respect for each other—the right to become educated and to unfold oneself to the fullest of one's ability to serve God and men, the right to have at least enough to keep body and soul together, food and clothing and shelter, and medical care.

I have often felt terribly discouraged when arguing with our Congress in Washington about aid to the poor and abandoned of this world. They are counted in the billions, and many hundreds of millions of them are under the age of five and will never see the age of six. Often, I look around the room, and discover I am the only Catholic fighting the fight that the least of our brethren have more food or more education or the barest human essentials for human dignity. I would guess I could take a vote in parts of Louisiana where I had civil rights hearings years ago, and I could have got almost 100 percent of the Catholic population there to vote against abortion, but these same such people stood up and yelled insults at poor blacks who were trying to register to vote and to be human citizens in the country of their birth. I would guess you could take a vote in Boston tonight and get a very close to 100 percent vote from the Catholics on abortion, and yet those same people without any sense of the incongruity of it all will yell "nigger, go home"—sick at the thought that maybe their nice white child will get his education or her education at the side of a nice black child. I think it's a terrible thing that all around this world life is degraded for people unborn and for people born and doomed to die very soon. If we really want to convince the world and our country that we have respect for life, we had better start showing respect for life and the justice that should attend the promise of life for every human being—black or white or Western or Oriental or rich or poor, young or old—and we had better start saying that we are for the right to life in its flowering as well as its birth in every part of this world and in every part of this country. And we should indicate our willingness to uphold the right to life everywhere we go and in everything we do and that we will vindicate that right even at any personal sacrifice that might fall upon us to give.

The problem with this issue is that it has become in too many cases a Catholic issue—a negative issue, a restricted issue—and it should be as broad as life itself and it should carry with it the fulfillment of the promise of life in all of its parts, in all of its manifestations. It should be attended to the life of the old as well as to the life of the young, the life of those hundreds of thousands of children who will not reach the age of five after a dismal, miserable life as well as those who will never see the light of day. We have to somehow enlarge our vision and our respect for the mystery of life in each of its forms, and we can't on the one hand clamor against abortion and on the other hand rebel in acts of violence or stand still while billions of dollars are being wasted to create engines of destruction. We cannot go to the movies or watch television and revel in people murdering each other or support that great art form of the cowboys and the

Indians where the Indians always get killed by the cowboys and everybody cheers and the story ends happily.

Life is so violent today in so many forms. Human life is so depreciated and denatured in so many ways that if we want to really convince our fellow Americans that we respect the right to life then I think that we are going to have to change many of our judgments and many of our actions. And we have to show that we respect this right across the board for everyone, right across the board from the conception to the end of life, and we have to be more concerned about the poor and about those suffering injustice here and abroad, those deprived because of our conspicuous consumption. We have to somehow call ourselves out in every way possible for human life in every form and then people will begin to say, "They really mean it . . . they really believe it." It's not just a little narrow crusade that they are going to fight for this while closing their eyes to that. They are going to be concerned about this great mystery of life and cherish it deeply, whether it is in a poor ghetto child or a child over in the Sahel who has a bloated stomach. Whether it's an old person abandoned, a wino on the south side of Chicago. Whether he's black, Oriental, white or poor or young or old. They really respect life. They really are against violence. They really are against anything that brutalizes that enormously beautiful mysterious gift of life.

And I think too that it will have something to say about our attitudes toward sex, because you know there is so much today that is bestial and dehumanizing about the beautiful concept of sex which in a sense is the portal of life, the means by which life was created on the human scale to prepare the material for God to infuse with an immortal soul on the eternal scale. Somehow we have to resurrect our own respect for sex and for life, viewing with mystery and awe the creation of life itself through sexual activity.

I think one of the great manifestations of the respect for life is celibacy, because one of the great gifts that all priests offer to God when they lay flat here on this floor to be ordained is the power to create life and to collaborate with God in that creation—the most beautiful, the most eternal creation that takes place on earth. And I think that great gift is great because of what it means and what is given and the symbolism of it, of giving oneself to everyone else in giving up that great gift while receiving the power to nurture others in eternal life which is born in us at baptism and grows throughout our life, our life in grace.

I would think, my dear friends, that we have a lot of thinking to do and a lot of stock to take if we are going to look ahead the next two years, the next ten years, the next twenty years and see the mentality of this country changing. We must believe in and respect life deeply enough to respect it wherever it is threatened and under whatever conditions it is threatened. Until then I don't think that we are going to win this argument with our fellow citizens. I don't think that we are going to persuade them that we really believe it. And I think that every time Catholics stand up and say something or do something miserable with regard to human rights anywhere in this country or in this world, they are disqualifying themselves to even open their mouths regarding respect for life. Respect for life is a beautiful human trait, but we have to nurture it across the board, not just in this narrow channel.

I would like to leave with you a thought that has occurred to me very often as a way of speaking to other Americans who are generally fair and open-minded. While all of us are terribly emotional on this issue, I think we are not going to solve it with emotion as much as by reason and civility and understanding and humanity. It is what we do that is going to speak much louder than what we say. And if we have established our credentials of respect across the board, then I think we have a right to speak for respect for the life of the yet unborn. But to respect the one and to close our eyes to the atrocities afflicting the other is, I think, to disqualify us from saying anything at all.

I stood once outside a Chinese cemetery in Hong Kong and across the portal of that cemetery was a Chinese inscription, and I asked the gentleman I was with what it said. And he said it's a very curious, old saying. It says, "What you are I once was.

What I am you soon will be." It seems to me that that message from one end of the spectrum of life—from the dead—can be matched by a similar message from those at the other end.

And it might help us to understand the problem if it were said to us tonight from all the yet unborn. When they say to us, "What I am now, you once were. What you are I shall somehow sometime be." But whether or not this happens for millions of people, I think, will depend upon how well we can portray to others who disagree our deep and abiding respect for life, our willingness to help the unfolding of its mystery in the whole world around us, the generosity with which we are open in our profession of this respect by the use of our own life, by our powers of procreation, by our sensitivity to all of the issues of violence and hunger and bestiality in our day. I think to the extent that we accept life willingly this night from God's hands as all of us have, to that extent we respect that higher life within us that he has given us over and above our temporal life. And if we take this to be the patrimony of all those yet unborn and especially the patrimony of those already born, then I think we shall think more deeply of life, we shall certainly respect it more deeply and I think we might also defend it more effectively. God bless you all.

Homily at the Law School Red Mass
Sunday, October 1, 1978

. . . The Gospel for today's Mass is a shocker—as are many gospels if we read them carefully. Jesus is addressing the chief priests and the elders of the people. And he gives them a case.

The father in the story asks his two sons to go to work in his vineyard. As lawyers you all have received this call to serve justice, especially where it is ill served and might be better served by one seized by a passion for justice. The first son glibly says he is on his way, but he really never starts. He professes, but he does not practice. He is an also-ran who does not run.

At least the second son is honest. He does not glibly accept the task; he is no idealist; he does not profess to serve. He simply says, "No, I will not." But then, he had second thoughts. The Gospel indicates a conversion. He regretted his unwillingness to serve. He then went and did what was expected of him.

What is the point of the story? Herein lies the shock. Jesus was speaking to those who professed to uphold the Torah, the law. They were the chief priests and the elders, but they were performing badly. Justice and the compassion mentioned by Paul in the second reading was hardly their compelling passion. They made a mockery of the law, dividing its purity into impure minutiae, legal skullduggery, nit-picking insensitivities, self-serving escape clauses, anything but justice for the poor and oppressed, surely profit for themselves and the powerful.

Conscious of their public profession and obvious commitment to the Torah, to justice, Jesus asked them, "Which of the two did what the father wanted?" What his Father wanted of them, justice, is the obvious meaning of this question. Were they, the leaders, really working for the grandeur of the law, justice, the coming of his kingdom on earth?

They were trapped. Yet, they were bright enough to state the obvious. The second son, reluctant at first, saw the light and did at last what he first refused to do. He worked for justice in the kingdom. He served the law. He was obviously the better son.

Now, gently but firmly, Jesus presses home the point to those committed to justice, but who, in fact, were serving themselves, not the oppressed.

In this post-Nixonian age, I wish we could find another translation to the one that begins, "Let me make it clear." Jesus does though make it clear to these leaders. John, the Baptist, came preaching holiness—for them it had to be a passion for justice that was their profession. They put no faith in John. They did not really believe in justice, although that was their profession, their only way to holiness. No, they preferred to serve themselves, to profit from their position, to obfuscate the Torah, the law, not to clarify it and to make it truly serve justice. Rather they used their legal gimmickry to ease the burdens for their friends, the powerful of their world, and likewise added burdens to the oppressed of their day, the poor, the widows, the orphaned, those suffering injustice. And so, like the first son, while professing to serve the kingdom, to do the will of the Father, in fact they served injustice and falsified their public profession. In another part of the Gospel, Jesus calls this by its true name, "Woe to you, hypocrites."

Now comes the ultimate shocker. To confront them with the magnitude of their dereliction, before justice and the law, Jesus picks the oldest of the professions, the prostitutes, and the most disreputable, the tax collectors, and identifies them with the just one, the second son, who said no to the invitation and then later regretted his decision and said yes. The prostitutes and the tax collectors listened to John's call to holiness and believed in him. Adding insult to injury, Jesus says to the chief priests and the elders, "Even when you saw that, *you* did not believe in him."

Jesus then makes perfectly clear what the story means, what the point is that he is making, "Tax collectors and prostitutes are entering the kingdom of God before you."

. . . I am sure that, with the inspiration and help of the Holy Spirit, this company will be more perceptive to the message of Jesus than the chief priests and the elders were. Your profession, your invitation to both the service of justice and concurrent holiness is, I trust, seriously heard and followed. You will not say yes and stay home. You may hesitate at times, so do we all and so did the second son. But let us today say yes, heartily and enthusiastically, to do what the Father wants of us for his kingdom: that justice be served through the law and through the work of those who profess justice, that holiness may be possible to each of you because of this service, and that his kingdom may come, in our time, through your efforts.

Remarks at Ecumenical Service Following Signing of the Peace Treaty
Lincoln Memorial, Washington, D.C., March 26, 1979

The Christian reaction to the events of this day must be one of unalloyed joy, happiness, and deep satisfaction. If religious persons are committed profoundly to one simple reality all around the world, it must be to *peace*.

Our Lord's final words, the night before he died, were spoken of peace, during a Seder, a Passover meal, in Jerusalem.

If anyone loves Me, he will keep My word, and My Father will love him, and We shall come to him and make Our home with him.

Peace, I bequeath to you, My own peace I give you, a peace the world cannot give, this is My gift to you. Let not your hearts be troubled or afraid (Jn 14:23, 27).

Once more, after thirty long years of prayer and negotiation, he has again given us peace in that precious part of the world where he was born, in Bethlehem, Egypt to which he fled from Herod, Haaretz, Israel, to which he returned, and where he lived, worked, prayed, died, arose again from the dead, and ascended to his Father. To what two nations on earth might his peace more appropriately belong tonight? He lived in both of them, loved them and their peoples, made them sacred by his presence and his life, his words and his works.

He also said, that same night before he died, "I have told you all this so that you may find peace in Me. In the world you will have trouble, but be brave, I have overcome the world" (Jn 16:33).

May we ponder his advice tonight, may all our great leaders who have elaborated this peace ponder his advice: "Do not be troubled, do not be afraid, be brave." It is our faith in God that gives all of us courage, strength, and peace.

It may not have occurred to you as my two Brothers, Mohammed Abdul and Rabbi Rabinowitz, were speaking earlier, that we three represent three remarkably allied religious faiths.

We all believe in one God—Allah, Elohim, and in his peace.

We are all three religious of the Book—religions based on a written revelation, the Old Testament, the Koran, the New Testament, all written in this same part of the world, all speaking often of the treasure of peace. In fact, both Muslims and Jews greet each other with this very word—peace, Salaam, Shalom.

All three of us hold Jerusalem, a name which means the City of Peace, to be a holy city. Who can forget the psalms of David that were written there ("If I forget you, Jerusalem, may my tongue cleave to my palate, my right hand be forgotten" Ps 137). The long history of the Jewish people has been centered in Jerusalem, even during long centuries of exile when they said from all over the world, "Next year in Jerusalem"—a cry of hope and anguish. Who can forget the Wailing Wall, the honored dead who lie in peace nearby? The Muslims cherish Jerusalem for the Mosque of Omar, the Dome of the Rock—the third most blessed place on earth—from which the Holy Prophet ascended into heaven. And for us Christians, who can ever forget the Holy Sepulcher, Golgotha, the Garden of Gethsemane, the Via Dolorosa, Bethlehem, Nazareth, Galilee.

For all three of us, this is a holy land, in a way, the umbilical of the world, the area from which some of our most cherished religious beliefs originate and find their home—like the Ten Commandments in the Sinai.

At last, for Egyptians and Israelis and their blessed lands and peoples, peace has come, peace, the blessed fruit of vision, courage, and generosity, on the part of Sadat, Begin, and Carter. May we thank God this night for the blessed outcome of their common efforts, this peaceful answer to all our prayers.

May we also now remember well that peace is not just the absence of war, but a frame of mind, an attitude that is best expressed in the ancient Latin adage, *opus justitiae pax*—peace is the work of justice.

Peace we have tonight, but peace we will maintain only by works of justice, that as the Koran, Isaiah, and the Evangelists say, we must feed the hungry, give a dwelling to the homeless, take in the stranger, help the widows and orphans, in a word, do justice to all those who suffer. Without justice, especially to the poor, the homeless, and the hopeless, there will be no peace.

All our three religious faiths are agreed in this: We best serve the one Holy God, we best maintain peace, we best love our neighbor, by giving ourselves to works of justice throughout these lands which have cradled the best and the worst of mankind's endless struggle to attain peace at last.

Now that we have peace, we pray to Our God to inspire and to help us nurture this peace and to deepen its blessings in all of our lives by committing ourselves to justice.

May I conclude with a prayer for my fellow Christians that was offered at Mass yesterday throughout the world. It seems especially appropriate to this special open moment in the long and often weary history of our times:

Let us pray.

God Our Father, your Word, Jesus Christ, spoke peace to a sinful world and brought mankind a gift of reconciliation by the suffering and death he endured. Teach us, the people who bear his name, to follow the example he gave us: May our faith, hope, and charity turn hatred to love, conflict to peace, death to eternal life. Through Christ, Our Lord. Amen.

As-Salaam-Alaikum, Shalom, Peace, be with you all.

Homily for Dedication Mass of Notre Dame London Law Center
July 29, 1983

My dear friends:

The first reading, which Sean Concannon read, is fairly simple. We don't have to go to the highest heavens to look for the law because it really is innate within all of us. We all have our sense of what is right and what is wrong and what is just. We have that inner voice that speaks to us, and we call it conscience. It is hard to hide from it, and it is almost always there when we need it. There is something inside us which is a call to justice.

But going beyond that in speaking of the Gospel story today, we see another quality of the lawyer, one that is not always there and *is* always needed. If you were to ask me, "What would you want the law faculty to do?" I would have to say, "Turn out competent lawyers, lawyers who know the law, and who are competent in doing their job." But if you ask me, "Is that enough?" I would have to say, "No." The lawyer who spoke to Jesus in the story we just read did us a great favor because he asked him, "What do I have to do to be saved?" The Lord's answer was simple and Socratic. He said to the lawyer, "What do you think?" And the man said quite truly, "You have to love the Lord your God with your whole heart, your whole soul, and all your mind and your neighbor as yourself." And Jesus said, "You are right. Do that and you will be saved."

But then the lawyer wanted to get the last word, and asked, "But who is my neighbor?" And Jesus told that wonderful story of the Good Samaritan. Now the story is simple, and I don't have to retell it. But I can explain, I think, something of what it means. If you have ever walked down the road, as I have, between Jerusalem and Jericho you go down through a deep and winding valley with high hills on both sides. The land is seared and hot, much hotter than it is here. As you go down that dusty road, you can also see the new superhighway which the Israelis have built. The old road is hot and dusty and twisting down to the Dead Sea. A short distance from the road's end is Jericho, a beautiful little oasis about eight hundred feet below sea level. Well, the man got set upon, not unusual for us today—a man gets mugged, beaten up, robbed, stripped of anything worth taking, and is left bleeding, probably naked, certainly penniless, there in the hot sun by the roadside.

It is interesting that Jesus said that the first person who went by was a priest, because he kept on walking. He did not want to get involved. He could see there was a problem, but he sidled over to the side of the road and slid by without even going near the person who was injured and wounded and maybe even dying and helpless. Next was the Levite, a member of the priestly class in Israel. He, too, did not want to get involved. His reaction was similar to those who pass an accident on the toll road or highway. They don't want to get involved so they slide by and hope the guy makes it who is lying on the side of the road in a wreck of a car. Doctors do that; lawyers do that; priests do that too, sometimes.

But then comes the Samaritan. He is very carefully chosen because the Samaritans were the Negroes of that day, despised by the majority. Jesus makes it the Samaritan who looks at this poor, wounded fellow and is moved to compassion. He stops, and he goes over, and he does what he can do with the fellow. He pours in wine, the only disinfectant he's got (at least it has some alcohol in it), and he pours in the oil to try to soothe the pain of the wound. And it is a long way down that little road through those hills, and he puts the man on his own beast of burden while he walks.

He does not take him to a local hospital or call the Red Cross; there isn't any such thing. He takes himself to the only place you can take a person in that shape—to the inn, the caravansary. He takes him and says, "Do what you can, I have to go on, but here is some money to take care of it, and I will stop on the way back, and if it costs more, I will take care of that, too." And Jesus asked the lawyer, "Who was his neighbor?" and he said, "The one that was moved to compassion."

I would have to say to you that it is not enough to know the law. There are a lot of marvelously trained lawyers who are paid enormous fees for very competent work. But with 600,000 lawyers in our country today, as against 15,000 in all of Japan and practically none in China, one would think we could not possibly have all the discontinuities of justice that occur in our cities, in our states, and in our nation. You would think that no one would really be suffering because of his or her rights not being vindicated.

A lawyer has to have something more than just competence, because he or she is a professional person, and a professional person is at the service of those in need. If you are a priest, you have to have your antennae out to people who need help for salvation, nourishment for their souls. If you are a doctor, you have to be open to people who need help in their health and their physical well-being. If you are a psychiatrist, you have to be sensitive to those who need to restore their mental well-being. And, if you are a lawyer, you have to be on the side of those who are suffering injustice, who are denied the human dignity they were born with, who don't have their rights respected as they should be, who are oppressed and powerless.

You don't really come through as a professional person—as a lawyer, or a doctor, or a priest, or a psychiatrist, or a teacher—unless you are compassionate, unless you suffer with those who suffer, and unless you are open to those who need your help. That is what makes you a professional person, being there to serve those who need you, whether you get paid for it or not. Now you say that is crazy, that is idealistic. It may be OK for you, Father Ted, because you don't need the money. But I say to you that if, as a lawyer, you go through your whole life and you never stand up to defend justice; if you can't reach out to the poor, the powerless, the minorities who need help; and if you don't have compassion, you are not a neighbor. Nor are you really a good professional person. And you may not save your soul.

None of you has seen God—I have not seen God—but we all see our neighbors around us, suffering, poor, and in need of us. And if we walk by because we don't want to get involved or there is no money in it to justify the hassle, we may be successful as lawyers in Chicago or New York or San Francisco or Atlanta or New Orleans, but we will not be professional persons or good Christians. Actually, we will not even be good lawyers, because a lawyer cannot be separated from his or her professional commitment, and our professional commitment is to people.

I have been impressed by some very good lawyers I know who always have time to step out of their regular practice to take care of someone who is being passed by, someone whom everyone is walking around, to the right and to the left, leaving them lying in the street. I think these are the people who love God the only way we can love him—in our neighbor, in the ones we see, the least brethren. If you go through your professional life only serving the most brethren, it is not going to be anywhere near as satisfying as you might think. One of our Deans used to tell his students, "If, at the end of your professional life as a lawyer, justice has not been better served or accomplished in your time or if people are still in great numbers suffering injustice because no one is there to vindicate them, you have not been a very good lawyer."

So today at this Red Mass we can pray to the Holy Spirit for all kinds of different gifts. If I were a young lawyer, I think I would pray for a sense of justice. I would pray that I had the courage not just to spend a lot of time studying the law, but also to spend the rest of my life learning it better. Beyond that, I would want to ask one more thing. I would want to ask the Lord to give me a sense of compassion, to say, "Lord, don't let me walk by the people who need me. Don't let me sidle off to the side of the road and slide by, as though I don't really see it. Give me the sense to be the Samaritan, to be touched with compassion at what I see. Give me the generosity to step in and do something about it. Lord, let me love you in your least brethren, because that is the only way I can, and let me be a great lawyer because

I do something, whatever I can, wherever I am, to make justice a reality in my day." May we all pray for that today, each one of us in our own way.

PART VII

LIVES WELL LIVED

> May all of your lives, today and every day, be
> living sermons to those with whom you live. And
> may all of you, with God's grace, persevere unto
> the end in doing good.
> —*Fr. Ted Hesburgh, CSC*

What does a Christian life well-lived look like? As is evident by
the diversity and vibrancy of the communion of saints, reflective of the full vibrancy of humankind, no two lives lived well
will ever look the same. At the end of life, each of our lives will
necessarily look different in light of the time, talent, and treasure
with which each is uniquely entrusted for their season on earth.
However, young or old, rich or poor, to live well is to "live every
day close to God" in surrender, in service, and in search of His
truth. In short, a life well lived is the life of a faithful baptized
beloved dedicated to prayer, learning, and action within one's
divine calling. Such daily intimacy with one's Lord bears in the
life of a believer the fruit of selflessness, peace, generosity, gentle-
ness, and hope. In God's economy, the faithful are called to some
degree of sacrifice, yet with the wondrously fulfilled promise of
life abundant and life everlasting.

This concluding section is made up largely of excerpts from
eulogies and funeral sermons celebrating the lives of those who
walked in obedience and love. Some ran businesses ("Homily at
Funeral Mass for Bernard Voll"), some had families ("Eulogy at
Funeral of Dr. George N. Shuster"), and some, it could be said,

died before their time ("Notre Dame Men—Father and Son"). Even as Fr. Ted's words highlight the best of these earthly lives, there emerges his undeniable belief in the wholeness and glorious unity with Christ promised to His faithful. While those who have gone before enjoy this radiance of God's eternal presence, those on earth simultaneously long for Heaven and live well their committed lives of faith, justice, and truth.

Notre Dame Men—Father and Son
January 30, 1955

There will be a final day in all of our lives. What will it be like? Largely, I think, like the rest of our lives. Our final day on earth will probably reflect the values we hold today, the strength of our character today, the closeness of our union with God today. In reflecting these, our last day will indicate to God and to ourselves the kind of eternity that awaits us.

. . . Some of you good listeners are fathers or mothers, all of you belong to a family, some of you are young sons and daughters. You may not be wealthy, or even healthy, you may not be handsome, or beautiful, or brilliant, you may not have a high position in this world or a fascinating future before you. From an eternal point of view, none of these things are really important when your life is finished and your last day on earth begins. All that matters then is how you stand with God, how well you have used whatever talents or position in life that God did give you. . . . If you live every day close to God, it does not matter how or when or where you die—for the person who lives with God has nothing to fear in time or in eternity. Ask yourself then this morning—am I living today in such a way that I could meet God tonight and not be ashamed of how I am living? Of the life God gave me?

. . . May all of your lives, today and every day, be living sermons to those with whom you live. And may all of you, with God's grace, persevere unto the end in doing good.

Funeral Sermon for Arch Ward
July 12, 1955

Every minute of every day, someone is born and someone dies on earth. All of us take much of this for granted as we pass through the middle ground of our own lives. Occasionally, a birth touches our family and we share for a few moments the hopes that attend each new life that begins. Then, too, suddenly a death occurs in our circle of friends and we pause for a moment to assess a life that has been and is no more on earth.

This pause that we share in common this morning is good for all of us, even though it is mingled with sadness and sorrow. The very sadness and sorrow testify that here is a life that was good, a human presence that will be missed. Every life, our own included, carries with it a great potential for good or evil. If we so often leave the good unrealized in our lives and become enmeshed in evil at times, perhaps it is because we do not pause often enough to assess our own lives, to ask ourselves where we are going, and if the days of our lives add up to something good, something that will be missed when our lives are finished.

You see, there will be a day when for each of us the sands of life run out, when God, the Giver of life, will ask us what use we have made of our talents, when our families and friends will look at our record, as we are looking at this man's record today. We need not fear for him. His work is done, at least, almost done, for he has one last task to perform for us this morning.

. . . St. Thomas Aquinas once said that there are only three really important endeavors in life: to have faith in the right things, to hope for the right things, to love the right things in life. You could summarize all of our lives, and Arch Ward's too, by looking at the things he had faith in, hoped for, and loved.

. . . Here, then, is the sermon that Arch Ward preaches to us and to the world today: that every life has eternal value if a man will have faith in, hope for, and love the right things; that everything good in life is a means of bringing us to the knowledge and love and service of God; that no other kind of life is really worth living, for as St. Augustine has said: "Thou hast made us for Thyself, O Lord, and the heart of man is restless until he rests in Thee."

Sermon at the Dedication of Saint John Church and Catholic Student Center, Michigan State University
January 12, 1958

Sometimes a man's life may seem to be a failure by worldly standards, but if he has followed truth and dedicated himself unselfishly, with all his mind and heart, to what he perceives to be the will of God, failure cannot possibly be the ultimate measure of his life, no matter what happens to him.

Eulogy at Funeral of Mr. Charles Jones
December 12, 1970

Peace is part of every concept of eternity because our lives and time are so frantic, frenetic, and un-peaceful. Hope leads us to look ahead with confidence in God's wonderful saving grace that, if we are doing our best to follow the law of love and generosity and friendship freely given, somehow this will perdure eternally, and we with it. If good does not perdure, life is a nightmare and this world a madhouse.

Eulogy Delivered at Funeral Mass for I. A. O'Shaughnessy
November 26, 1973

There are many ways of testing a man's life: how well he does in reaching his goals, presuming them to be both high and noble; how he affects other people for good or evil; how faithful he is to his basic principles; how high his hopes; how loving his heart; what good works he leaves behind; how happy his memory. By whatever calculus you judge a man, these tests or other ones, including the simple Christian test of loving God and one's neighbor, I. A. O'Shaughnessy was a good man who lived a good and a long life and died a good death in the Lord.

I would like to memorialize I. A. O'Shaughnessy today according to another test, equally simple and yet quite profound. One of the greatest theologians of all times, St. Thomas Aquinas, said that a good man is one who knows the right things to have faith in, the right things to hope for, and the right things to love. How did I. A. O'Shaughnessy meet this test?

He basically had faith in God and in all that he judged to flow from God as from its source: His truth—the Christian message, not selective parts of it, but all of it, however difficult at times. He had faith in God's Church and he did faithfully, even generously, whatever the Church demanded of him, and was more than generous with whatever he judged to be the Church's works— especially the needy ones. He believed in Christian education to the extent that two of its better known institutions, St. Thomas here in St. Paul and Notre Dame in Indiana, found in him their greatest among many great benefactors. He believed in God's special servants, priests and brothers and nuns—and he loved to be with them, to help them, to kid them, to laugh with them. He had faith in people, especially people in trouble, and God alone knows how many of them he helped in a thousand different ways. He had faith in his family, especially enjoying their joys and shouldering their sorrows which he made his own. He had faith in his friends, and they were without number, over many years and in many different lands and throughout our land and they never needed him or his friendship in vain—he was there. He had great faith in God's Providence which saw him through almost ninety years of vicissitudes without end, some good and some bad, but all deepening the inner strength and solidity of his character, as granite is given ever more clearly the definition of the sculptor by each mark of the chisel. When God is doing the sculpturing, as I. A. believed to be the case in life, the result is both Godlike and goodly. Thus was his faith.

What did I. A. O'Shaughnessy hope for? I know he always wanted what was good for his wife and children and their children, and he always put this above and beyond what he hoped for himself. Like all of us, he hoped for success in life, but his hopes went far beyond material prosperity, although he had plenty of that. He hoped to be able to do good for others and dedicated his material success to that end, more than anyone I have ever known. I know he hoped for heaven, too, and was willing to pay the price to get there suffering more than most people knew, without ever complaining about the personal and physical pains that came his way in regular abundance. His hopes were both good and elevating.

It is not difficult, if you knew him well, to see clearly what he loved. First, God and the service of God as it was given to him to serve. He loved all of God's creation, too—good people who delighted him, especially women and children and youngsters with bright eyes and high hopes. Somehow he was always young with the young, never really old and stuffy. He loved life and laughter, a good game and a good joke, a good day with a brisk wind on the sunlit Florida waters or a moonlit night of sailing on the great lakes. He loved being with his family and friends, loved giving away most of his income each year, loved getting others to give when they really did not want to, and loved surprising those in need with a sudden solution to their seemingly impossible problems. He loved to vacation for a few days with his priest friends, and he attended each of their Masses in turn during the pre-concelebration days. I never spent a single day with him that he did not serve my Mass and receive Holy Communion with sincere devotion. When his eyesight failed, he used to ask me to read my breviary out loud so that he could ponder and enjoy this prayer of the Church. As I was away from the University, I did not know that he was dying the day he died, but that morning as I was offering Mass at St. Patrick's Cathedral in New York, it suddenly occurred to me out of the blue that it might be nice to offer Mass for I. A. that day and I did. I have to believe that this good inspiration came from the good Lord I. A. had served so

well and so long, as a way of speeding him on his way home, as
he began his last day on earth. As we live, so shall we die.

Eulogy at Funeral
of Dr. George N. Shuster
January 28, 1977

The difference between those who truly believe in Our Lord and
those who do not is that believers live in hope of eternal life, and
it keeps them traveling Godward through the long, tiring, and
trying days of their lives which are also lived in love.

What do we really learn from the long life of this great and
gentle man to whom we bid good-bye today? What did he really
have faith in, hope for, and love?

Those of us who were privileged to work with him and know
him well were strengthened in our own faith just by being with
him, watching him, listening to him. His faith was a rock to
which his life was anchored, a North Star keeping him on the
right path through life, an inspiration that was evident in everything he did. In the words of the Gospel, he was the faithful
servant of everything that was good.

. . . God only knows how many crises I and others brought to
him, as to a Father Confessor, who listened sympathetically and
always gave wise counsel. Like a good gardener, he brought out
the best in us, all the beauty and goodness that we did not know
we had until he discovered and encouraged it in us. While he
was a quintessential layman in a rather clerical church, I always
saw in him a priest, a mediator who stood between ignorance
and learning, badness and goodness, promise and fulfillment,
always bridging the gap, always leading upward.

I know a once dreary Catholic university in South America
that is bright and shining today because he cared enough to go
there often, with great personal sacrifice, and to show them the

way. I know of discouraged and defeated scholars who came to life because he beckoned the way to do it and gave them a gentle push. I know so many students who were losing faith, not only in God, but everything else, who found in his staunch and unwavering faith the means of recovering their own. As an educator, they are perhaps his best monument. I know of frustrated priests who were ready to call it quits until he opened to them new and exciting vistas. I know many young and old members of this community today who instinctively call him Father, and I am one of them. He engendered faith and hope and love because he lived to the fullest these great virtues that lead us to God.

There is a wonderful line in the prayers for the dying—"Go forth, Christian soul, to meet your Savior and Lord." It seemed almost superfluous to say that to George in his final hours. He spent his whole life doing it. It was the substance of his faith and hope and love. He found the good Lord everywhere, sought and served him everywhere, found him in us and in our hopes, left us so much better because of this deep faith and hope and love that he lived among us.

Homily at Funeral Mass for Bernard Voll
September 23, 1981

As we read in Ecclesiastes, there is a time for birth and a time for dying. What is more important is what happens in between: the building, the loving, the laughter and tears, the healing, the dancing, the embracing and mourning, the war and the peace.

What Do You Want from Life?
No Date

What do you want from life?

There are many who would answer you. First, the obvious answer from Madison Avenue, which I trust you do not take too seriously, the trappings of the affluent society: food and drink—martinis and charcoal-broiled steaks from your very own backyard grill; the status symbols: house, sports cars, vacation spots, clothes, gadgets, hobbies, and the money to make all these possible. Material security and success, pleasure and ease, fun and games, so the litany goes. There is nothing wrong, of course, in the material amenities of our day. But to make their acquisition and enjoyment the end all of human existence is a folly worth avoiding like the plague. Too many people spend their lives on this narrow, inane track today and retire all too early to become vegetables.

To take a more serious approach to an answer, you might ask yourself, what are your values? I take it we might assume that these values are of a spiritual character, and that they represent what you really intend to live for and work for or, if need be, to suffer and die for. These values are what you must use to define the kind of person you wish to be, the kind of life you intend to live, the best hoped-for meaning of your life in the days ahead, however many or few they will be.

You must make up your own list, of course, for you must live your own life for your own goals. But I would like to suggest some of the enduring values that have made human existence worthwhile in every age, and that could make your life most meaningful in our times. Beyond that, these values also share the fine patina of eternity, for they have withstood the test of time. They have endured through every crisis that man has known.

First of all, *commitment to truth* in all its forms: the joy of ever seeking truth, the peace of finding truth everywhere, the courage of living truth always. Open-mindedness is the prelude to this commitment, intellectual honesty is its truest spirit, and purity of life is essential to both possession of the truth and commitment to what it demands of us.

Commitment to what is good and excellent. I mean here no narrowly selfish good, but that every good and noble inspiration might find in you a champion and a defender, and indeed a personification. What is good for your own moral integrity, yes, but also the realization that you will often find yourself and your good in spending yourself and your talent for the good of others who need you. To avoid the taint of intellectual and moral mediocrity, to be willing to stand for something, even something unpopular, if it is good; to be willing to be a minority of one if need be, this is part of the commitment. But not to be a neutral where principle is involved, a moral cipher, a pragmatic compromiser who easily takes on the protective coloration of whatever moral environment happens to be at hand. This is also ruled out by commitment. Is it too much to expect of you? Anything less is all too little.

A *passion for justice* in our times. Again, not merely justice for yourself, or your family, or your profession, but especially a passion for justice as regards those who have few friends and fewer champions. There are great and festering injustices in our country and in our world. You can sidestep them if you wish, you can close your eyes and say it is none of your business. Then remember that freedom and equality of opportunity in our times are quite indivisible. If one class, or nation, or race of men is not really free, then the freedom of all men is endangered. Injustice breeds more injustice, disorder begets more disorder. You do not need a suit of armor, or a white horse, or a sword, but just a sensitivity to justice wherever it is endangered, a quiet passion to be concerned for justice in our times, a compassion for all men who suffer injustice, or the fruits of injustice.

Lastly, I would suggest a value that could have many names, but the simplest name of all is *faith.* Faith is not an easy virtue for those who in their own profession instinctively take nothing on faith. But in the broader world of man's total voyage through time to eternity, faith is not only a gracious companion, but an essential guide. Faith begins with belief in God, he who is, the ultimate eternal Source of all else that is; all truth, all goodness, all beauty, all justice, all order. Science, as science, tells us nothing of this, nor does science deny any of this, unless you take seriously the prattling of Cosmonaut Titov about not seeing God while in orbit.

Faith: I take it to be a gift of God, but one that is amenable to rational foundations and prayerful preparation. It is not just a blind leap into the dark on no evidence whatsoever. It is rather a luminous opening on another world that adds new personal dimensions to one's life and wider vistas to one's highest endeavors. For these reasons, I have added faith to my list of the values that make life more meaningful. A lifetime is not long enough to cherish such values, nor is eternity too long to reward them.

"Come, Holy Spirit"

Come Holy Spirit,
fill the hearts of your
faithful and kindle in them
the fire of your love.
Send forth your Spirit
and they shall be created.
And you shall renew
the face of the earth.

O, God, who by the
light of the Holy Spirit,
did instruct the hearts
of the faithful, grant that
by the same Holy Spirit
we may be truly wise and
ever enjoy His consolations,

Through Christ Our Lord,
Amen.

INDEX

Fr. Theodore Hesburgh, CSC (1917–2015), was a theologian, public servant, and the fifteenth president of the University of Notre Dame, serving from 1952 to 1987.

He is considered one of the most influential figures in higher education, national and international affairs, and the Catholic Church in the twentieth century. Hesburgh would say, however, that his only vocation was to be a priest. "The happiest day of my life was when I was anointed a Catholic priest," he said.

Hesburgh was ordained a priest of the Congregation of Holy Cross in 1943 and celebrated Mass almost every day after that. As president of Notre Dame, Hesburgh is recognized for opening enrollment to women in 1972, increasing minority representation in the workforce, doubling enrollment, and increasing faculty salaries, student aid, research funding, and endowment to the university.

Hesburgh is the recipient of 150 honorary degrees, a Guinness World Record. He was given sixteen presidential appointments and he served on the International Atomic Energy Agency, the National Science Board, and the Civil Rights Commission. He joined Martin Luther King Jr. at a civil rights rally at Soldier Field in 1964, an event memorialized in a now-iconic photo and statue of the two men holding hands.

Among his many awards and honors, Hesburgh was bestowed with the Presidential Medal of Freedom and a Congressional Gold Medal.

hesburgh.nd.edu

Todd C. Ream is a professor of higher education at Taylor University.

Hannah M. Pick is the program manager for the Dundon-Berchtold Institute for Moral Formation and Applied Ethics at the University of Portland.

Fr. Gerard J. Olinger, CSC, is the vice president of student affairs at the University of Notre Dame.